The **DRUMMOND HILL CREW** Series:

Boyz to Men
Livin' Large
Age Ain't Nothing But A Number

   The author, **Yinka Adebayo**, is a London
school teacher. He wrote the Drummond Hill
Crew books to give his young pupils "something they would relate to...something they
would enjoy...something to think about."

The **DRUMMOND HILL CREW** Series

boyz to men

Yinka Adebayo

The
X
Press

Published by
The X Press, 6 Hoxton Square, London N1 6NU
Tel: 0171 729 1199 Fax: 0171 729 1771
e-mail: Xpress @ maxis.co.uk

Distributed by Turnaround, Unit 3, Olympia Trading Estate,
Coburg Road, London N22 6TZ
Tel: 0181 829 3000 Fax: 0181 881 5088

Printed by BPC Paperbacks Ltd, Aylesbury, Bucks.

ISBN 1-874509-29-8

CHAPTER ONE

"Hey Darren, what's wrong?"

Darren James turned to see his best friend running across the playground of Drummond Hill Comprehensive, a broad grin on his face.

"Why have you been dissin' me lately?" Tyrone asked in a concerned voice. "I was waiting for you at break time as usual and you never showed up."

"Am I my brother's keeper?" snapped Darren remembering a line from a movie, the name of which he couldn't recall. "I need my own space at times."

Tyrone looked over at the group of Year 10 boys leaning against the school gates. He had seen Darren talking to them earlier. Everyone knew about them. They acted as if they were cool, and always ended up in detention for smoking cigarettes or getting into some other trouble. But Darren seemed not to have noticed that. He had this spaced-out look about him these days, thought Tyrone.

"Darren, what's up, man?"

"What's up?" said Darren in amazement. He gave Tyrone a playful cuff on the back of the head. "You ask me what's wrong after you give me a mouldy cheese sandwich at lunch time. What do you expect?"

"Yes, but you know me," Tyrone replied, "I'm always clowning about."

"I know," said Darren and went to give Tyrone another slap. Tyrone saw it coming

2

and ducked, just in time. "It's not really the sandwich, it's just that I've got other things on my mind. Anyway, how can I stay mad at you when you're coming round to my place tonight to help me with my revision?"

"Oh, yes," Tyrone mumbled, more to himself than to Darren. He hoped that he didn't sound too disappointed. One thing he realised was that he didn't really have the time to do both his work and coach Darren for the maths test tomorrow. But he hated to say 'no' to his best friend. That was the thing with having someone looking out for you, thought Tyrone.

As the boys walked towards the bus stop along the tree-lined avenue leading from their school, Tyrone thought about his problem. How was he going to make the time?

The short walk to the bus stop was one that he and Darren had made every day since they started at Drummond Hill. They knew every inch of the way. In fact they even knew how many steps it was from their school gates to the bus stop. 1,476.

Tyrone had his right arm around Darren's

shoulders as they walked; from his left shoulder hung a bag. Darren's bag swung from his right shoulder. Their school ties were cut short and tucked into their shirts in the latest style, and each sported the same black patent shoes.

Darren couldn't really be described as handsome, but neither was he ugly. He had tight curly hair shaped into a high-top style and lips that curled upwards at the sides giving the impression that he was constantly smiling. His eyes were large in a friendly, dark face. Looking at him there was no reason to guess at the existence of his greatest asset — a sister of startling beauty.

Tyrone, in contrast, was shorter and slimmer than his friend. His hair was less compact, but styled in the same manner. His light-skin complexion, light eyes, dimpled cheeks and almost straight nose were inherited from the father he had not seen for almost a year.

The boys had been best friends for almost eight years.

The large semi-detached houses on the

road leading to the bus stop all had freshly cut lawns, some neatly adorned with weeping willows. Others, like the house with chrysanthemums, were bordered by rows of spring flowers such as daffodils and early Dutch tulips.

"Did you see Duane Edwards in music today?" asked Darren suddenly, his eyes wide open. "His haircut was just mash up. He looked like one of the Jackson Five!" Darren grinned broadly, his perfectly formed white teeth gleaming in the sunlight. The gap in the middle of them enhanced his cheeky persona.

"Leave him, Darren," said Tyrone, "it's not that bad. Anyway, maybe he can't afford to shave his hair as often as you do yours."

"Yeah," complained Darren, "but you must admit he really showed us up when we were doing that Jodeci number. Group ballads like that are supposed to be sung with everyone in the band looking criss."

"Darren," Tyrone said in exasperation, "you're so vain."

"I know, but one day, when I'm on Top of

the Pops, you'll be selling my story to the newspapers."

Darren became excited as he thought of himself as a famous singer. In his mind he heard the TV presenter announcing: "...and here he is, boys and girls, the latest sensation to hit the charts — Daaarren James!" He could see it clearly, the screaming girls, the big cars. He knew he had the talent. After all, he had come second in the talent competition at the youth centre last summer.

Tyrone, head bowed, was also thinking of the day Darren had sung on stage. He had felt so proud of his best friend as he was belting out the tune. He had cheered the loudest and the longest when Darren had performed. Seeing and hearing his homie hitting the high notes in front of the rapt audience felt almost as if he had been up there himself. This was the thing with Darren and him, they always wished the best for each other.

"And what about me?" Tyrone asked, looking up.

Darren gave a mischievous grin. "You can

be my driver or barber or something," he said with a wave of his hand.

Tyrone did not answer, choosing instead to stare down at the pavement. Darren said the most hurtful things at times.

They turned the corner and waited at the crossing for the traffic lights to change. When the green man came on, the boys walked across the road towards the bus stop.

The bus was late and there was already a bunch of school kids waiting at the bus stop. Darren and Tyrone joined the throng of noisy children jostling for position in the queue.

Tyrone leant with his back on the bus shelter, his hands dug deep into his pockets. Darren faced him. Out of the corner of his eye, Tyrone could see Robert Collins, a kid in Year 7, receiving a kick from two of the boys he'd seen with Darren earlier. Robert let out a yelp of pain as he was made to hand over some money to his tormentors.

Darren's face changed as he remembered something. Fishing into the inside pocket of his blazer he pulled out a packet of wine gums and popped one into his mouth. He looked up at his friend who was licking his lips expectantly. He wondered whether he should share his sweets with Tyrone, but decided he didn't have enough to go round.

"Guess what?" Tyrone said suddenly.

"You're a monkey and I'm not," Darren replied laughing. He saw his chance to put the sweets back in his pocket while Tyrone's mind was occupied.

"No, serious," Tyrone said. He had noticed that Darren had not offered him a wine gum, but didn't care. They only stuck in your teeth anyway. "Mr Singh's asked me to edit the Year 8 magazine. You could do an article for it."

"Shane Rollinson will be better at that, he's always lounging about," replied Darren.

"You could do a piece on computer games," continued Tyrone, unfazed by his friend's reluctance. "Sonic the Hedgehog, Street Fighter — break time will never be the same again!"

But Darren wasn't listening. The bus had arrived and he was wondering why it was that buses always seemed to arrive in groups. He was still thinking about it as he ran towards the last one; the way he figured it, that was the safest bet for a seat. Most of the other kids were pushing and shoving to get on the first bus, a few had dodged past their mates and had managed to sit down on the middle one, but very few of the pupils had bothered with the third bus which was almost empty. As he ran, Darren took a quick peek over his shoulder to make sure that Tyrone was following. Luckily he was.

"About the magazine," Darren said as he flashed his bus pass at the driver. "I don't think I'll bother."

Tyrone was a little out of breath, but eventually managed to speak. "You mean you don't want unlimited access to the computer room at lunch time?" he asked incredulously.

Darren shook his head slowly. "I've got better things to do with my lunch breaks," he said in a low voice.

Tyrone tried not to look too disappointed. He and Darren always did things together.

"Anyway, I think you're missing out," Tyrone said. It wasn't like Darren to pass on such an opportunity and he knew that better than anyone else, because they had been best friends since the age of four. He remembered how he had first met Darren.

It was their first day at the nursery. He had been playing with his Action Man and his favourite red racing car when Darren was dragged screaming and kicking into the reception class by his mother. Tyrone had taken to him straight away, after all he had been in the same situation only a few days before. Being a kind-hearted kid, Tyrone had offered Darren his shiny red car to play with. Darren had immediately fallen in love with it and had even taken it home after class. In fact, he still hadn't given it back to this day!

Only Tyrone and Darren were left on the bus as it approached their stop. The two boys ran down the stairs and only just managed to get out of the doors before the driver closed them.

Darren frowned, his brow screwed into a knot. "You know, you're always moaning," he said to Tyrone as they ambled along the leafy pavement.

Tyrone was hurt. Darren didn't seem to understand that he was only thinking of him. He wanted to share any success that he might have with his mate. "If you say so. I'll see you at six," he said in a quiet voice. They had reached the junction where they always parted company to go home.

"Yeah, see you at my place at six," replied Darren hurriedly.

The boys gave their secret handshake before going their separate ways. "Respect," said Tyrone before Darren turned left up Acacia Avenue.

As Tyrone carried on up Wood Lane, he passed the old corner shop. It had stood empty for as long as he could remember, so long in fact that people had started to put posters up on the windows. Every so often someone would come along with a big bucket of glue and paste new ones on. He and Darren would often try to guess which new poster would be going up. Today there were no new ones.

The rest of the buildings on the road were red-brick, pre-war terraced houses that went along the road for a hundred yards or so on both sides. The rows of privet hedges that lined the front of the houses were designed to give the street a countryside feel. But to the residents, the bushes were a means of hiding yourself from inquisitive eyes. Tyrone would sometimes wish that his street was as smart as those on the route to his school. In contrast to Drummond Hill, his street was littered with boxes, newspapers and empty beer cans, courtesy of the local drunks and travellers who camped by the disused recreation field.

The problem was made even worse by the way the refuse collectors always seemed to leave most of the contents of the bins in the road when they came by.

As Tyrone walked, he couldn't help but think about Darren's behaviour earlier. Something seemed to be worrying him, but he couldn't make out what it was. Over the years he had become quite an expert in spotting when his friend had a problem. It would usually be something trivial like having to go shopping with his mother when he would rather be playing soccer for the school team. But very occasionally it was something more serious, like the time that Darren had broken his mum's favourite vase whilst playing basketball in the living room. They'd spent ages trying to fix it.

The boys' friendship had strengthened over the years, especially when both their mothers found summer jobs at the local play centre and, instead of paying babysitters, took their children along to work with them.

While their mothers were looking after the other kids, the two friends would be left to find something to do. That was usually the signal for them to get into some sort of mischief, like the time when Darren had declared, "Let's play terminators!" and they spent the rest of the afternoon charging around the play centre and darting through the jungle of toys.

Then Darren had decided that Tony Marshall and Robert Collins, who were busy minding their own business, were trespassing on his and Tyrone's territory. He suggested attacking them and Tyrone agreed.

Everything would have been fine if Darren hadn't bent Robert's finger back so far that he started to holler in pain. Tyrone winced painfully as he remembered the licks he got from his mother that day. Afterwards, the two friends had named it 'the lost battle'.

Tyrone stopped outside one of the red-brick terraced houses about half-way down the street: he was home. He paused momentarily outside before opening the black wrought-iron gate. There was a pushchair outside the front door. Tyrone recognised it. It was the one he had sat in as a baby, the one his brother now used. Tyrone sighed as he ran a finger along the side of the buggy. His mother must have forgotten her own advice about how you can't take any chances of leaving anything lying about in this neighbourhood. He knew she was right, after all hadn't Errol Carpenter got his bike pinched when he left it unguarded for five minutes outside his house last week? Errol had been inconsolable when he realised that it was missing.

As he entered the house wheeling the

pushchair into the hallway, Tyrone threw his bag under the stairs. He could hear his mother, Marcia, talking to his baby brother, Aaron, in the living room. "I'm home, Mum!" he called as he kicked his shoes off. He poked his head into the living room. Marcia was on the floor pointing out pictures in a book to the gurgling baby. Aaron looked up and smiled. Tyrone poked his tongue out. His brother laughed.

Marcia looked up. "Hi baby, how was school?" she asked.

Tyrone mumbled a reply under his breath and turned and ran the few stairs up to his room. He didn't have time today for any chit chat with mum, all he wanted was to do his work so that he would be ready for Darren later on that evening.

Meanwhile, Darren had gone home in an angry mood. The questioning that Tyrone had put him through earlier had confused him. All he could think of was the conversation he had had earlier on with Marvin

Johnson and the rest of the Smokers' Corner Crew about the possibility of a vacancy in their gang. Darren envied the Smokers' Corner Crew. They were so cool.

Darren's house, in contrast to Tyrone's, was rather elegantly situated and furnished. His road was an exclusive cul-de-sac with a park and golf course backing onto his garden. The house itself was a detached four bedroom with a mock Tudor front and a large front garden. Two stone lions on the front walls guarded the house. Tyrone would often cycle over to Darren's and they would have fun in the park or play a round of mini-golf, always paid for by Darren's parents, of course.

Darren didn't mind paying for Tyrone when they did things together. He understood that Tyrone's mother was having a hard time lately and that she couldn't afford to give Tyrone pocket money on a regular basis.

Darren went into the kitchen where his elder sister, Patricia, was sitting by the dining table drinking a can of Diet Coke and chewing gum. She had a pair of headphones wrapped around long flowing dark hair that she hot-combed every fortnight. Her green eyes glistened through the contact lenses she wore. She looked up as Darren entered and flicked a peanut from a jar onto his head.

"Aargh!" grunted Darren angrily. "What do you think you're playing at?"

Patricia didn't seem to hear or care, but carried on listening to her head-set, nodding rhythmically to the music.

He kissed his teeth.

Darren couldn't stand his older sister. She was in Year 10 at Drummond Hill and always had the boys flocking after her. She was forever using the phone and spent endless hours in her bedroom. The only advantage that Darren could see in having a sister was that he never got bullied by any of the older boys because they all fancied her. Last year the boys in 10C had voted her the most fanciable girl.

Darren poured a glass of milk from the bottle on the table and rolled his eyes in over-exaggerated exasperation as he looked over at Patricia miming to a song using her hairbrush as a microphone. He left the kitchen and made his way up the stairs to his bedroom and turned on his stereo.

"Come on Darren, you've got to concentrate," pleaded Tyrone. He had arrived at Darren's house as promised but had been cheesed off at himself for being late. Tyrone hated to be late.

His lateness was all on account of Tenisha Markham, a girl in their class. Tyrone had met her on the corner of Wood Lane and Acacia Avenue as she was running an errand for her mother. Tenisha had kept on about how she had a sore throat but Tyrone had found that hard to believe. If she had a sore throat, how come she kept on talking so much? He only managed to get away from her when her mother poked her head out of the window and asked her why she hadn't gone to the shops.

"Don't you want to revise?" Tyrone asked Darren. He picked up Darren's school blazer which was lying on the floor. He was getting increasingly irritated by Darren's attitude. It was now almost 7.00 and his friend was just lying there looking up at the ceiling, day dreaming. That wasn't all; his room looked like a bomb had hit it. "You knew I was coming," Tyrone said, raising his voice slightly. "The least you could have done was start swotting."

Darren kept on staring up as he lay on his back with his hands behind his head, seemingly in another world. He wished that he didn't have a test the next day and that somehow Tyrone could learn everything for him. All he wanted to do was hang out with his new friends.

"And look at the state of this room," Tyrone said with a wave of his arms.

One thing that got up Tyrone's nose was untidiness. It wasn't as if his friend had a lot of clearing up to do. Darren's room was much larger than his and contained all the latest gadgets. Two computer consoles and a writing desk were placed by the window and a wall to wall cupboard covered one side of

19

the room. Posters of top footballers were stuck above the pine bunk bed. Nevertheless, Darren had the annoying habit of always leaving things lying about on the floor.

Darren sat up and looked at Tyrone as he picked clothes up from the floor. Tyrone was starting to sound like Mum, thought Darren to himself. Compared to his new Year 10 friends, Tyrone was a real wimp.

"I just can't figure you out at times," Darren said in an important voice.

"What d'you mean by that?" asked Tyrone, surprised.

"Well, we just do the same things all the time. You never want to do anything exciting or daring like we used to."

Tyrone was hurt at his friend's comments. He opened his mouth to speak, but decided against it. It seemed to him that Darren was in one of those moods that he seemed to be having lately. "Listen," Tyrone said, picking up a notepad and pencil, "we're supposed to be swotting up for the test. Are you ready?"

Darren grunted a half-hearted reply and picked up a pencil.

They had been revising for over half an hour but Darren's mind was not on the work. He could only make out bits of what his mate was saying: "...Right angle...decimal point...when you multiply move it to the right". His mind was racing. All he had on his mind was the Smokers' Corner Crew.

"Darren, wake up!"

Darren jumped up, startled. "Yeah," he mumbled.

Tyrone was sitting on the edge of the bed, textbook and pen in hand, looking straight at him.

"You haven't heard a word I've said, have you?" Tyrone asked.

"Yes I have."

"Well, if you haven't, you'd better pray for a miracle if you expect to pass," Tyrone said, folding his arms in resignation.

Darren knew that Tyrone was right as usual. He was saved from explaining himself when he heard his mother's voice calling both of them down for dinner.

At dinner, Tyrone was going on about how he had been given the task of editing the year magazine. Darren cringed. He knew where the conversation was heading. Next, his mother would be asking about home-work and stuff.

"That's very nice," Yvonne James said, "your mother must be really pleased with you."

Tyrone shifted in his seat. "Yes," he replied, in a confident tone, "she has promised to help me with the design of the front cover. I've also got Anton Powell and Tenisha Markham to help with the articles."

"Yeuck! Anton Powell and Tenisha Markham, the most 'butters' kids in the whole school," grunted Darren under his breath.

Yvonne spun around, an angry look on her face. Darren tensed for what he knew was about to come next. He recognised that look on her face. He only hoped that he wouldn't be grounded.

"At least they are getting on with their school work," said his mother in a sharp tone, "unlike you lately, my young man."

Darren turned to look at Tyrone. He had

known that it would turn out like this. One thing that Darren couldn't stand about Tyrone these days was the way he went about bigging up his chest as though he was so smart; the way he crawled to his mother telling her how well he was getting on and stuff. He was forever getting compliments from Darren's mother, whereas the most Darren got from her was an, "All right, but you could do better". Anyway, all that would change soon. He was sure of that.

CHAPTER TWO

Darren woke up early the following day. He had not had that much sleep during the night. He had been too excited about the special meeting of the Smokers' Corner Crew he had been invited to. Not just anyone was invited to their meetings, you had to have some special talent in order to be asked along. The excitement of all that the invitation meant was so much that he had tossed and turned all night from thinking about it. It had taken him ages to get any sleep. It had got so bad that he had had to get out of bed and do twenty press-ups on the bedroom floor. By the time he had managed to get some shut-eye, it was almost daylight.

Yawning, Darren made his way downstairs. He knew he was going to miss the bus that morning and wondered why he hadn't heard the alarm on his radio going off.

As he entered the kitchen, dragging his feet, he groaned to himself when he saw his mother seated by the breakfast bar. She was a tall, slim, dark-skinned woman who, even at this early hour of the morning, had already applied her make-up, though she still wore her frilly pink dressing gown. Yvonne had an anxious look on her face as she watched Darren approach her. Unlike her husband, who regarded outward displays of emotion as self-indulgent and only for wimps, she was a warm, tactile individual. Her friends regularly confided in her and knew that they could be sure of a welcome smile, a relaxing cup of tea and a shoulder to cry on. She was always at home. Yvonne had stopped work the year before and sometimes found it hard to find things to do during the day.

Her life these days was a long way away from her upbringing, near the beach front in Ocho Rios, Jamaica. Yvonne's introduction to life was into a world of affluence and power. Growing up she had everything a spoiled child could wish for. Her father, a top politician of the time, would pander to any of her whims. An expensive private school at the age of twelve, instant admittance to all the best parties from the age of fourteen, an expensive open-topped sports car at seventeen. She had had it all. Then at eighteen she met, fell in love and married Lester, Darren's father. He was a medical student when they met at the fashion show in Kingston. The show had been held in her honour by one of her friends, a fashion designer. The young couple had come to England soon after so that Lester could complete his studies.

Although he didn't at first earn half as

much as her father in Jamaica, Lester supported his wife, and the daughter they had soon after, well.

Yvonne furnished the house in the same style as she dressed, which is to say very tastefully. The house was antiseptically cleaned and dusted every day. Her model-like posture brought out the best in the dog-tooth-check hobble skirt suits that she wore on the weekends. Unlike her main girlfriend Marcia, who never gave in to the excesses of fashion, and whose motto was 'If you really find something that suits you and never lets you down, stick with it', Yvonne enjoyed dressing elegantly and adventurously. She stared at her second-born as he rubbed his sleepy eyes.

"You must have had cotton wool in your ears last night."

"What's that?" asked Darren.

"What sort of time do you call this?" Yvonne asked raising her voice.

Darren shrugged his shoulders, he couldn't figure out why she always asked him stupid questions. She knew very well what the time was, so why was she asking?

"You've got to pull your socks up, Darren James," she said.

Darren's face screwed up into a scowl. He turned to walk out of the room, not wanting to remain in the same vicinity while she was mouthing off.

"Mum, don't ride me," Darren said as he stopped at the door. "I've got a maths test today and I don't want to miss the bus."

Yvonne James looked at the disappearing back of her son. It was not like Darren to be hurrying to do a maths test. She promised herself that she would speak to his father about him later on.

Darren ran out of his house and up Acacia Avenue as fast as his legs and heavy school bag would allow him. When he reached Tyrone's street, he took a quick glance round to check if Tyrone had waited for him. He wasn't around. Darren hadn't really expected him to wait this long. He increased his pace and continued on towards the bus stop, hoping that he hadn't missed the bus. If he had, the next one wasn't for half an hour and that meant he'd be late and would be due for Mr Singh's detention class. As he approached the junction, he saw the bus about to pull away. Darren panicked.

"Wait for me!" he shouted in desperation, waving his arms frantically in the air hoping that the bus driver would notice. The bus slowed to a halt; the driver must have seen him because the doors at the front slid open invitingly. Darren sprinted a little faster.

"Respect," he said to the driver as he finally clambered onto the bus. He offered the man his fist in greeting, and shrugged his shoulders when the driver paid him no mind.

The bottom deck was packed tightly with noisy chattering pupils and the odd adult. Most grown-ups purposely missed the early morning bus and either waited for a later one to arrive or else would take a leisurely walk to wherever they were going. They reasoned that you had to have a screw loose to put yourself through the ordeal of screaming kids and books thrown with great force at sculpted hairstyles which, if they connected, would surely do someone a serious injury. And all this before nine o'clock in the morning.

Darren looked around nervously before he tried to push his way through the jam-packed bodies. This wasn't easy as no one was prepared to make way for him. There were shouts from his school mates. "Easy nuh! Where do you think you're going?" and "Ouch!!" from a small Year 7 boy when Darren accidently trod on his toe.

The digs that Darren was getting in the ribs reminded him of a game he used to play in primary school called Bulldog, where you had to run through a gauntlet of punches and kicks. He finally saw Tyrone standing by the crowded stairs.

"Upstairs," Tyrone said, jabbing a finger skywards.

There was a group of older boys standing blocking the sanctuary of the top deck. The look on their faces told Darren that his intended passage to safety was going to meet the same result as the previous mêlée. He braced himself ready for what he knew he had to do. Head first, he charged into the bigger boys. He knew he would get a few Chinese burns and dead legs before he could get up the stairs. In his haste he knocked into a greying old lady seated near the middle doors. His bag hit her on the knees.

"Well, I never!" she complained, revealing a loose, yellowing tooth as she spoke. She seemed to be chewing on it, but Darren couldn't believe this was true.

"Oh, sorry," Darren apologised.

"No manners, that's what I say," she grumbled, chewing rhythmically.

By the time Darren reached the top of the stairs Tyrone had saved a seat and was waving from the back for Darren to come and join him.

"Hey bro', I thought you were going to miss the bus today," he said to Darren.

"So did I," said Darren, a little out of breath from running for the bus and all the beatings he had suffered on the sardine-like deck below.

"Are you ready for the test today?" Tyrone asked, as he turned to face Darren.

There was a noise coming from the back of the bus and Darren turned his head just in time to see a bag sailing towards him. He saw Robert Collins, being shaken by Steven Corbin and Darryl Hall from Year 10. Tyrone made to get up, but a restraining arm from Darren stopped him. His eyes met Darren's, and he could see by the look that Darren gave him that he had better not get himself involved. Tyrone could see the sense in this, it wasn't his fight and all he might end up doing was getting himself beaten up. A quick glance at the other pupils on the bus was all that was needed to see that they were of a similar opinion. Everyone seemed to have embarrassed looks on their faces but no one wanted to get themselves involved.

There was a man, who looked like he was a builder, with a flat cap on, seated near where Robert was being tortured. The man stood and pulled Steven and Darryl away from the weeping Robert. Steven, brave as usual, shrugged himself free from the man's strong grip and wagged a threatening finger at Robert.

"Later!" he spat defiantly.

Robert Collins was saved from any further punishment as the bus pulled up at the stop near school.

By the time they reached the playground it was already swarming with pupils buzzing around excitedly. It was as if they were all trying to use up any excess energy that they had stored up from the night before. Today was like every other morning at Drummond Hill. The school was a popular one for parents from that part of town to send their kids to. It was set in a large area of green lawn and trees, with its own playing fields catering for everything from cricket to rounders, football to athletics. These resources enabled Drummond Hill to win a lot of the inter-school tournaments.

Darren and Tyrone walked through this early morning rabble side by side. There were some boys recreating the soccer match that had been on TV the night before. Over by the fences, a couple of boys had even started to argue about a dubious goal. Some girls were standing around discussing the latest gossip in their teen magazines. Others were peering expectantly by the school gates as they waited for their friends to arrive.

"Hi, Darren," a voice called suddenly above the din of screaming pupils.

Darren spun around to see Remi Oluseyi, a really pretty girl in his year. "Her folks have nuff dollars!" Tyrone was always telling him. Her mother owned the only West Indian take-away restaurant in town. Unfortunately, Remi thought a lot of herself and she often acted as if she were a super-model or something, always sashaying and mincing around the school as though she owned the place.

But Darren thought differently. He had often watched her in class and caught her looking over at him sometimes. He felt a hot flush rising up his cheeks, the way she was staring at him made him feel uncomfortable. Darren turned to Tyrone, "I think that Remi has got a handle on me."

Tyrone stared at his friend in a strange way. What could he possibly mean? Did Remi think he was a door or something?

"What!" he exclaimed. "But she's a girl."

"Yeah, I know, but you must admit that Remi is different."

"Jeez…what…?"

Tyrone didn't get a chance to finish his sentence because Darren suddenly started to jump up and down and wave his arms around.

"Hi!" Darren called out to Marvin Johnson and Roland Meade, both from Year 10, who were leaning on the wall by the bike sheds waving back.

"I've got to go," Darren said, excitedly, as he ran through the throng of kids.

Tyrone stood there for a moment, frustrated that Darren didn't want to be with him. Then he thought to himself he didn't really mind. After all, he had the magazine to organise. He peered towards the school gates and saw Tenisha and Anton walking in together. Anton was dragging his heavy school bag over the concrete floor as usual. Tyrone ran up to them.

"I've got something to discuss with you," he said, in a matter-of-fact way.

35

"Oh, goody," replied Tenisha. "What's it about?"

"I haven't got time to go into it now," said Tyrone hurriedly.

"Well, why don't we buck up together at lunch time or something?" said Anton.

Tyrone thought about it for a second. "Well..." he said, hesitating. He wasn't so sure what Darren would think if he invited someone else to have lunch with them. "OK, we'll meet here at lunch time." Tyrone hoped that if Darren saw him working with someone else, and saw how popular it was, he would want to be part of the magazine too. Maybe this was the way he could get them to do something together again.

The bell rang and after registration was school assembly. The majority of the pupils used the time between the two gatherings as an extension of their break. There was the usual shoving and pushing, and when Philip Hector, who was in a different Year 8 class from Darren and Tyrone, slipped and fell down on the floor, it signalled an excuse for the stampede they were looking for. One thing that you didn't do at Drummond Hill was fall over in the corridor when everyone was shoving. All the boys just carried on pushing, some were kicking and there was so much noise it was a wonder that Mr Fredricks, the headmaster, didn't come out of his office.

Darren remarked later on that Philip Hector might have died if Mr Singh hadn't come to his rescue and shouted at the top of his voice "Stop!"

Almost at once everybody was still. Mr Singh had that sort of effect on the lower school.

At assembly, Darren stood next to Tyrone. They were singing a hymn and Darren, as usual, tried his hardest to make Tyrone laugh — it was one of those hymns with a joke line in it.

We plough the fields and scatter,
The good seed on the land
But it is fed and watered
By God's almighty hand.

Darren replaced the words 'good seed' with 'gunga peas' and it caused them to break out into chuckles that only stopped when Mr Singh glared at them.

The first lesson was history. Tyrone and Darren enjoyed this subject the most because their teacher, Mr Robertson, often gave lessons about the brave kings and queens of Africa.

Mr Robertson was a broad-shouldered Trinidadian whose kind, hazel-coloured eyes and commanding voice had made him one of the most liked teachers in the school. He had only been teaching for a year — Drummond Hill was his first post since qualifying — but he had not hesitated to bring radical thinking and personal experiences of oppression into his unique and enjoyable lessons. Mr Robertson firmly believed that his pupils should hear the stories of their ancestors as well as those of the Romans or the Greeks or the Anglo-Saxons and as a result his classes were always well attended, with hardly any pupils bunking off.

"All right, settle down now," said Mr

Robertson, as the last student took his seat. "As we're running ahead of time on our Gunpowder Plot project, today we are going to talk about one of the best known slave abolitionists of her day: Sojourner Truth."

All the pupils leaned forward — this was going to be a very interesting lesson.

During the hour Mr Robertson painted a picture with his words of Isabella Baumfree, or Sojourner Truth, as she later became known, that had his class on the edge of their seats. He described how Sojourner travelled throughout America speaking out against slavery, how her deep voice, quick wit and inspirational faith helped spread her fame. He described how she helped to find jobs and homes for slaves who had escaped from the South to Washington. His words flowed and painted a vivid picture of the harsh realities of being black a century ago. He had the class transfixed by his almost hypnotic words, everyone so engrossed in the lesson that they almost never heard the bell ringing to end it.

"Your homework tonight, which has to be

handed in next week," said Mr Robertson standing up, "is to write an essay on the life of a slave at the time of Sojourner Truth. There are some work sheets on the front desk to remind you of Isabella Baumfree's story."

With that he dismissed the class.

At lunch time, Darren and Tyrone rushed to the dinner hall. Tyrone grabbed two seats while Darren waited by the dinner queue. He returned a short while later with two trays and had just placed them on the table when he said, "Blouse an' skirt!"

"What's up?" said Tyrone wondering why Darren was speaking in Jamaican patois.

"I promised Marvin and Roland I'd sit on their table."

"But, Darren, this is our table, we always sit here, it's the closest to the dinner queue," said Tyrone, aghast.

"I know," said Darren in a matter-of-fact way.

"And it's the first table to get picked for second helpings!" said Tyrone, shaking his head in disbelief. He couldn't understand how Darren could throw away the chance of having a second round of jelly and ice cream just to sit with Marvin and Roland.

Darren stood there for a moment before picking up his tray.

"It's all right," said Tyrone, hurriedly looking at Darren, "I've got Tenisha and Anton coming in a minute. I need to discuss some things with them anyway."

Darren sauntered off, one arm dangling loosely by his side, to the other end of the dinner hall.

Tyrone looked at Darren walking away. He would rather talk to Tenisha and Anton than sit with the SCC, the Smokers' Corner Crew.

"At last," said Anton breathlessly when he arrived and plonked himself on a chair beside Tyrone. Tenisha was behind him, beaming, her eyes looking bigger than they were through the boffin glasses she insisted on wearing.

Tyrone thought for a second that perhaps Tenisha and Anton were butters, especially when someone in Year 10 who he didn't really know tried to squeeze past their table.

"Move out of the way, bigga," the older boy said to Anton when he couldn't get past. Tyrone expected Anton to react, but he seemed unconcerned at being called names and grinned sheepishly instead as he stuffed his mouth with a forkful of lumpy mashed potatoes.

Anton was shorter than most of the boys in their year and grossly overweight. Everyone poked fun at him because he was so fat, even the children in Year 7. Kids were forever coming up to him to grab hold of the loose flesh that hung whale-like on his stomach and make comments like, "The Michelin man has got a spare tyre!" Tyrone was always telling him to go on a diet, but Anton just didn't seem to have the will power.

Tyrone giggled to himself when he thought of how Anton used to come into the youth centre in his cut-off jeans and Pony trainers. He had looked really sad and everyone would poke fun at him. Then one day Anton had decided to buy a pair of the latest trainers, Nikes with the air bubble in them. Then he had come into the club with them on, swaggering and posing around. And before he knew it Marvin Johnson had got a pin and burst them, causing Anton to bawl and cry. Everyone else had laughed. That was when Tyrone had decided to become friends with Anton, because Marvin had been well out of order. He didn't need to do that in front of the whole youth centre.

And Tenisha...nobody in their class really liked her because she lied so much. She was always saying she was ill or that she had badly injured herself, but then you would see her running about on her so-called broken ankle. Tyrone didn't really mind her though. As far as he was concerned, Tenisha's problem was she craved attention.

"Right," Tyrone declared in a grand manner. "I've been given the task of organising the new Year 8 magazine, and I'm volunteering the both of you as my helpers."

Anton stopped, his fork midway to his open mouth.

"Great!" he said, grinning broadly.

"Do you have any ideas about what we could put into it?" Tyrone asked searchingly.

Tenisha leaned forward, her eyes were lit up.

"What about having a horoscope section?"

"Yes, and lots of posters of groups like TLC and Whitney Houston," Anton said, flicking his fingers. He really wanted to be involved in the magazine. As far as he was concerned, if he could be seen to be working with something so exciting and popular it stood to reason that he would make tons of friends. There were one or two pupils like Tyrone and Tenisha who talked to him, but he wanted everyone else to like him too.

Anton's eyes shone as he got increasingly excited.

"Yes, why not? I could be the roving reporter that travels all over the world interviewing pop stars," he said dreamily. "Do you think I'm getting carried away?"

"No, Anton," Tyrone answered swiftly. "Okay, pens and paper at the ready...let's get to work."

And with that the three of them set about

their task and started to scribble away in their notepads. They were still writing when Patrick Annette suddenly arrived and put his tray on their table. Tyrone placed his head in his hands. Patrick was the pain of their year and was forever shooting his mouth off about things he knew nothing about. He was the last person that Tyrone wanted to see.

"I know something you don't know," Patrick declared as he pulled up a chair.

"What's that then?" sighed Tyrone impatiently, wondering what sort of skank he was going to hear.

Patrick looked pleased that he had distracted the three of them from their work.

"Desmond Walker has been suspended for a month for going into the girls' changing rooms."

"You're kidding," Tyrone said, sitting up a little straighter in his seat. "How do you know?"

"You know how things stay," Patrick said, shrugging his shoulders. "I keep telling you I'm the main man." And with that he stood up and walked away.

"Wow!" Tyrone declared as he watched Patrick disappear. He couldn't wait to see Darren's face when he told him.

Over at the other end of the dinner hall Darren was sitting with five members of the Smokers' Corner Crew: Marvin Johnson, Roland Meade, Steven Corbin, Darryl Hall and Daniel Browne. Darren was feeling chuffed with himself. It was as though he was on stage, like the time when he sang at the youth centre. Loads of pupils kept looking over at him as he sat with his new friends.

He could see why they were staring. Steven, Marvin and the rest were the coolest. They had taken over the bike sheds and if you cycled into school you had to pay thirty pence a week to the SCC to leave your bike there. This was a 'tax', Marvin explained. He said that everyone got taxed eventually in their life and he might as well start them off now before someone else did. Even the girls

46

in Year 10 and 11 were looking over in their direction. Darren felt big. He felt proud that he had been asked to sit on the most important table. Seeing girls waving at them convinced Darren that he wanted to join them. As far as he was concerned, the SCC were the most popular group in school. If he was made a member he could hang out by the sheds any time he wanted. If he played his cards right they might even invite him to all the brilliant parties that he heard they organised every month.

He turned to Marvin. "So what now?" he asked.

Marvin finished his lunch without acknowledging Darren's question. When he was done, he pushed his tray away, rubbing his stomach in appreciation of the tasty meal.

"What do you mean?" he said, pushing back his chair.

"What am I supposed to do?"

Marvin took a quick glance at Roland. Darren couldn't be sure whether they exchanged sly winks or not. "I'm not sure whether you're ready," Marvin said importantly.

Darren panicked. "Yes I am," he said in a determined voice.

Roland stared at Darren in a way that sent a slight shiver down Darren's spine. "If you pass the test, then you'll be allowed to do anything you want."

"Seen," Marvin said offering Roland his fist.

"Like what?" Darren asked nervously.

"Well…" drawled Marvin as he patted down his skiffle haircut. He took a quick glance around him and leaned forward. "I suppose we can tell you."

"Going out with girls," Daniel Browne said, leaning across the table with a leer spreading over his face.

"Setting our own school rules," Marvin continued, his eyes twinkling.

"Yes," said Darren, becoming increasingly excited.

"The thing is, if you become a member, you'll be the same as us — an outlaw," Roland said dramatically.

"What do you mean by that?" Darren asked in a confused voice.

"We sit together and get caned together,"

Marvin said staring straight into Darren's eyes.

"We also hang out at the arcade on Preston Road," Marvin said with a flourish.

The arcade! That was the place where all the bigger kids went. Darren had been warned by his parents not to go in there. This was getting really exciting.

"We also pay taxes every week."

"What's that for?" Darren asked, a little confused.

"To pay for unforeseen incidentals," Marvin explained.

"That's right," Roland interrupted, "and we don't want the SCC getting too big. We're an exclusive club."

Damn! thought Darren inwardly.

"But," said Roland, as though he had read Darren's mind, "there is a spot open at the moment."

Darren held his breath.

"And we've been looking at you for some time now," Marvin said. "We think that you've got what it takes to be a member."

That was all Darren wanted to hear.

CHAPTER THREE

Darren was still walking on air when the bell rang for the end of lunch. He was heading for Miss Bird's maths class, which was situated on the second floor of the school. The corridors were already filling up with pupils lining up outside their form rooms, the boys lounging about on one side of the door and the girls on the other. The headmaster had come up with this system of lining up as a way to stop the congestion which always developed in the passageways between lessons. But like everything new, it did not have the desired effect. If anything, it only caused more traffic.

There was a lot of talking and arguing all along the corridors as Darren wandered carelessly towards his class. As he approached the classroom he suddenly remembered the maths test. His hand shot up to his mouth. Panicking, he searched his classmates' eyes for a clue as to whether they, like him, had refrained from swotting up the night before. He wasn't sure, but it seemed to him that the pupils who were streaming into class 8B were also dreading what Miss Bird had in store for them.

"All right, keep the noise down," Mr Williams said, as Darren made his way to his seat at the back of the class. The noise subsided almost at once. Like an instamatic camera. The pupils turned to focus their attention at Mr Williams, the deputy head teacher, as he stepped towards the desk by the blackboard. They all had the same question on their minds. Where was Miss Bird? She was their form teacher as well as their maths teacher, and she had been in school at registration. Mr Williams cleared his throat.

"I suppose you are all wondering where your maths teacher is today?" he asked, looking at their quizzical faces. Some of the class murmured in the affirmative.

"She's been taken ill, and as a result the test, which I know you were all looking forward to, has been cancelled."

"Hooray!!" cheered the class.

"All right, calm down," Mr Williams said, trying desperately to restore some order to his charges. "The test has been postponed until next week."

A disgruntled moan spread around the classroom.

Darren couldn't believe his ears, it was as if all his prayers had been answered. A week's grace!

After the final period, Tyrone went to the

school gates as usual to wait for Darren so that they could go home together. He was looking forward to telling his friend the news he had heard about Desmond Walker from Patrick Annette, and to going to the youth centre that evening with Darren. It was Tuesday today and that meant basketball practice.

Tyrone was still waiting well past the time that Darren would normally have come out, even if he had been kept in for detention. Tyrone, confused, stood outside the school wondering whether something had happened to his friend. Okay, Darren was usually late — but this was taking the mickey. Suddenly it hit him. Darren was not showing up because he had made other plans again and he hadn't even bothered to tell him. Disappointed, Tyrone picked up his bag from where it lay and trudged, head bowed, towards the bus stop.

Meanwhile, Darren was jogging towards the arcade with Marvin Johnson and Roland

Meade. He had forgotten everything else, including Tyrone. Where he was going was more important. The Smokers' Corner Crew was the only thing on his mind. Going down the High Street with his new-found friends gave him an extra bounce to his stride. He felt so happy just being seen with Marvin and Roland. The look on the faces of all those Year 7 kids as the three of them headed towards the arcade made him pleased that he was being made a member. When he saw Robert Collins' terrified face staring at him from behind a tree, it made him laugh. As far as Darren was concerned Robert Collins was just jealous because he had not been invited to the SCC's special meeting.

When they arrived at the arcade, a couple of the SCC were standing around, and Steven Corbin and Daniel Browne were leaning on the machines while Darryl Hall was playing pinball. In the background, a fruit machine was spitting out pennies as someone nudged a jackpot. Darren took a quick glance about him. He saw that all the members of the crew had their school uniform on, or at least part of it, but had removed their ties and thrown their jackets on the floor by the machines. All of them, without exception, had donned the same American football jackets and dark sunglasses which they carried in their duffel bags at all times. Darren's heart was racing.

Marvin led him by the elbow, over to the machines on which Daniel and Steven were leaning.

"Glad you could make it," Steven addressed Darren in an official voice as they approached. "We asked you here to our office to see how serious you were about the code of honour of the SCC."

Darren's heart beat faster. He didn't know why but he was really expectant of what he was about to hear. "Yes," he replied in a faint voice.

"You know that only the privileged few are allowed to join our organisation?" Daniel said dramatically

Darren's heart was really zooming now.

"Well, we've decided that you've got what it takes."

This is it, thought Darren to himself.

"But..." Marvin began with a wave of his

hand. There was a quiet hush from everyone around. In the background Darren could hear the distinctive noise of the Mortal Kombat machine, "we do have initiation tasks that you have to carry out to be a full member."

"That's right," added someone behind Darren. He couldn't quite make out who it was.

"What are 'initiation tasks'?" asked Darren croakily.

"Well, we set you three things to do which you've got to complete, no matter how difficult or unpleasant. After that we have a vote and decide whether you can be in our crew."

Darren stood up straighter when he heard this. "What do I have to do?"

"First, you have to let off all the extinguishers on the first floor landing of the school," Marvin stated in an emphatic tone. He walked around the pinball machines where Steven was now playing, too preoccupied with beating the highest score of the day, as usual.

"Then," Roland said as a smile spread across his face, "you have to take the Year 10 mock exam papers from Mr Henry's locker."

Mr Henry's locker! Darren could not believe his ears. How was he going to do that? It was known throughout school that Mr Henry never left his locker unlocked and always carried the key in the top pocket of his jacket.

"And what's the third task?" Darren asked, half expecting to hear something dreadful.

"You have to nick eight bars of chocolate, one for each member of the crew, from Mr Patel's shop after school — without getting caught."

"Arrgh!" shrieked Darren. "How am I going to do that? I've never stolen anything before."

"That's part of the fun," Steven sniggered. He kicked the pinball machine as he lost his last credit.

Darren almost fainted when Steven said this. Stealing stuff from shops didn't seem that much fun, especially if you got caught and were sent to prison for a hundred years or something. But he so wanted to be a member of the SCC.

CHAPTER FOUR

"Darren, you're really out of order!"
Tyrone said, as soon as he saw his friend at
the youth centre. "Where were you?" he
demanded.

"Oh no," Darren said, putting his hands
over his eyes. "I totally forgot. I bumped into
Marvin and Roland earlier on and I completely lost track of time."

Darren's face looked guilty. All he had been able to think about since he attended the meeting of the SCC was how he was going to carry out the tasks that had been set for him. The worry had made his throat dry and his lips were cracked. And as if that wasn't enough, it had completely slipped his mind that Tyrone would be waiting for him as usual after school.

"Yes, well," Tyrone scowled as he sat down on one of the benches which were lined up against the wall. "The least you could have done was let me know."

"Mmm," murmured Darren.

"Do you know that I waited for over half an hour?"

"Yes, I know, I'm sorry. Look," Darren said, hurriedly, "I've got these..." He produced a packet of cigarettes from his pocket. He offered one to Tyrone.

Tyrone shook his head determinedly, declining Darren's offer with a wave of his hand. He was livid when he saw the cardboard and cellophane-wrapped drug.

"What are those for?" he asked wrinkling

59

his brow.

"For smoking, what do you think?" Darren replied airily.

"I don't understand you at times," Tyrone said, shaking his head. "Do you honestly want to stink like an old ashtray?"

Darren turned angrily. "What do you mean by that?"

"All that nicotine and tar all over your clothes," Tyrone said, pointing at Darren's baggy jeans, "in your lungs...and even your hair." Tyrone's voice was becoming increasingly shrill.

Darren dismissed his friend's remonstrations. "Look," he said in a superior tone, "I haven't come here for your approval. Anyway, do you know what your problem is?"

"What?" Tyrone answered in a defensive tone. He wondered what Darren was going to say now. He was coming out with a lot of strange statements lately.

"You're still a little yout'," Darren said, shoving his friend playfully in the ribs. Tyrone, shorter and slighter than Darren, staggered slightly.

"Well, I don't know about that," Tyrone replied, running over to the basketball courts. "What I do know is that smoking those cancer sticks will make you get out of breath in a fast-moving game like basketball."

"Yeah?" Darren said as he ran over to join him. "Is that a challenge?"

"If you think so," said Tyrone, grabbing a ball from the back court. He bounced it a couple of times and ran towards the basket, throwing the ball onto the backboard. The ball hit the rim and slid through the hoop. Tyrone jumped up, punching the air with his fists. He let out a yell of joy that could be heard throughout the youth centre.

"Yes! Two points to Magic Tyrone."

The look on Darren's face showed that he was not too impressed. He caught the ball on its way down.

"That was lucky," he said as he dribbled the ball past Tyrone.

Stunned, Tyrone struggled to compose himself. "What was lucky about it? Don't you know it's all in the wrist?" he said, demonstrating.

He tried to get the ball back, but Darren shielded it from him well, his large frame and outstretched arm concealing the ball, while all the while he kept it bouncing with his free hand.

Tyrone finally succeeded in stealing the ball from Darren. He bounced it a couple of times before throwing it towards the basketball hoop. Darren turned in disbelief as the ball sailed over his head in a graceful arc and landed in the hoop with a swoosh. Tyrone couldn't contain his joy. He danced around Darren, flicking his fingers tauntingly and laughing heartily.

"What was that then?" he asked.

"Fluke!" replied Darren, kicking the ball away disappointedly. Then changing the subject he said, "Anyway, what do you think of that girl, Remi?"

Tyrone stopped laughing almost immediately and picked the ball up from where it had landed. Why was Darren asking such silly questions? He thought Darren felt like him when it came to girls. He didn't think much of them. As far as he was concerned they wore skirts and were always crying if they fell over, and they couldn't play football for toffee. That pretty much summed girls up, in his view.

"Unhh! What are you on about?" he said.

"Nothing," said Darren hurriedly. He liked Remi a lot but he wasn't ready to let on to Tyrone just yet. Tyrone might think he was going soft or something if he told him how he felt about her.

"I felt really sorry for Robert Collins this morning," said Darren, changing the subject again as he bent down to tie the laces on his sneakers. "I would hate to live his life. He's always getting distressed."

Tyrone frowned and stared at Darren for an instant. "But I thought that Marvin and his boys were your friends?" he asked. As far as he was concerned, beating younger kids up was all he could make out the SCC did with their time. That and taxing people to chain their bikes by the shed. They were well out of order.

Darren bit his top lip trying to avoid meeting Tyrone's stare as he stood up. "Yes, but I'm not into beating up people and all that," he said, grabbing the basketball from Tyrone.

"Oh," said Tyrone a little confused. Darren didn't seem to be making any sense at all. What was the point in hanging around with them if he didn't want to beat people up? They were known all over school for their antics. He was quite sure that Darren was losing his marbles; the guy wasn't thinking logically. Maybe the nauseous smoke that Darren was taking into his lungs had made a little detour to his brain.

"Come on, let's slam dunk some ball," said Darren. He wanted to get Tyrone's mind off any talk of the SCC. Tyrone's attitude proved that he was uncool; he couldn't possibly be invited to join the crew. No, you had to be cool to be in. And that was what he was, with a capital C.

He threw the ball towards the hoop from the three point line, willing it to fly in the same arc as Tyrone's skilful shot earlier. He tensed his body, preparing to celebrate, as the ball began to dip a few feet from the backboard. It hit the board with a thud and hovered above the hoop for what seemed an eternity before rebounding off it. Darren's face fell in disappointment. He kicked the ball away in frustration as it bounced towards him.

Tyrone turned to face Darren. "That was really unlucky," he said, patting him on the back.

"Yeah," said Darren sulkily. He shrugged off Tyrone's sympathetic arm wondering, fleetingly, whether there was something in what Tyrone had said about his smoking. After all, it wasn't every day that he lost to his shorter friend when they played one on one basketball. "I've had enough, let's go home," he said, in what he hoped was a bright voice. With that they left the youth centre.

CHAPTER FIVE

Darren woke up the next day not wanting to go to school. Today was the day of his first initiation task — letting off the fire extinguishers on the first floor landing of the school.

He showered, dressed and turned on his radio. Whitney Houston's I Will Always Love You was playing. Darren tried to sing along but when it got to the bit in the chorus where Whitney started to sing in a high voice he had to give up. He sounded like the cats that normally wailed outside his bedroom window during the night. He didn't care too much about all that soppy music anyway.

He gathered up the text books which he needed for the day from his well-stacked bookcase and packed them neatly into his bag. He was nervous as hell. He knew from the start that sneaking out of any class was near enough impossible without someone being suspicious. How was he going to set off the extinguishers before anyone realised? What if someone put two and two together and worked out it was him? His father was sure to give him some licks if it came out. He rubbed the seat of his pants as he thought of the pain that would surely come if he got found out. "Cho," he said to himself, "I will not get caught. I will set off the fire extinguishers, I will show Marvin and the rest that I'm also a bad bwoy."

He gathered up his bag and headed off to

school. He had purposely decided to catch the earlier bus so that he could meet up with Marvin and the boys. As for Tyrone, he knew that his friend would go off to school on his own if he didn't see him at the stop.

When he got to school he saw Marvin and Roland standing by the bike sheds. Roland was smoking a cigarette. Darren went over to them. The playground was already teeming with noisy pupils and Roland had to speak up to make himself heard.

"How do you feel?"

"I feel confident," lied Darren. He looked down and saw that Roland's fingers were yellowing from where he held his cigarette, and every time he opened his mouth to speak he could smell the stale odour of nicotine and tar. His stomach turned as he moved his head out of the path of the reeking odour. Roland puffed at the cigarette a couple of times before blowing out a cloud of foul-smelling smoke. He raised his hand to his face as if to fan away the smoke but decided against it. He was sure that if Roland saw him doing that he would probably box him in the ear.

"That's the way to be, hang loose, easy, cool," Roland said in a dopey voice.

Tony Mensah, a well-known and much-feared heavy in Year 12 walked past them. Marvin watched the prefect's burly frame from the corner of his eye and Roland shifted his feet nervously, hiding his cigarette behind him.

Darren's mind raced. What if Tony had seen them? He'd most likely confiscate the cigarettes, put them on report and send them to the Head's room. He breathed an audible sigh of relief as Tony walked out of sight.

"I can't wait to see the look on all the teachers' faces," cried Marvin excitedly as he took the cigarette from Roland.

Darren wondered how Marvin failed to notice Roland's oral hygiene problems as he stood there letting the full force of his breath waft all over him.

"There is one little thing though," said Darren biting his bottom lip and turning his face slightly away from Roland.

Marvin eyed him suspiciously. "What's

that?" he asked, as he took a drag on the cigarette and let out a rasping cough as he inhaled.

"I need one of you to help me with something."

"Nah," said Marvin, "we're not allowed to get involved in any initiation tasks."

Roland took a few steps forward so he faced Darren and grabbed him by the collar, their faces almost touched. He headbutted Darren on the bridge of his nose.

"Are you trying to pull out?"

Darren shook his head slightly as he fought back the tears. The pain of the headbutt and the smell of Roland breathing all over him made him feel sick. Uggh!

"Is it getting too hot for you?" asked Roland, gritting his teeth in a menacing manner. Marvin placed a restraining arm on his friend's shoulder, just as he moved closer to thump Darren.

"What I need," continued Darren, ignoring Roland, "is a little distraction just after break time."

"No can do, Darren," said Roland flatly.

"Why don't you ask to be excused so that you can go to the toilet or something?"

"Okay, I guess you're right."

By the time Darren got into the geography class after break, Mr Jones, a thin, tall, bespectacled man, was already in his chair. The Toupee, as he was more commonly known amongst the pupils, shuffled the papers on his desk and looked up over his half-rimmed glasses at Darren as he ambled into the room. The Toupee let out a groan. If there was one thing he couldn't understand lately, it was the behaviour of Darren James. He was convinced that Darren had set out to make his life a misery. The last week especially had seen a big change in the boy's behaviour. Darren had started to forget his homework and begun distracting other pupils by talking to them. And The Toupee was also convinced that Darren was the culprit who put a drawing pin on his chair and a cockroach in his desk drawer. He took a quick glance in the drawer to make sure that the boy hadn't decided to play the same prank on him today. He let out a sigh of relief when he saw that the drawer was empty. If there was one thing that made his skin itch it was hairy-legged spiders and hard-backed roaches.

The Toupee straightened his tie and adjusted his ill-fitting brown corduroy trousers. He watched Darren suspiciously as the boy made his way between the desks and found a seat at the far end of the class.

Mr Jones had got his nickname 'The Toupee' because of his hairpiece. Patrick Annette had sneaked into the staff room one day and seen him putting it on. News of this discovery quickly spread through the school, and Mr Jones was now the butt of all their jokes. Although no one actually called him The Toupee to his face, he had known for a long time that his false hair, which seemed at times to have a mind of its own, was a major reason for the laughter in some of his classes.

The Toupee flicked open his textbook and said, "I have no doubt you all remembered that today is your deadline to finish the project we started a couple of weeks ago. By the end of this lesson, I want all completed projects handed in." He looked around him, pleased at the reaction that his question was having. He couldn't help but let out a little chuckle to himself as he gazed at all the nervous looks. He knew that a good proportion of the class would have forgotten about his deadline. It was pay back time for those snivelling, nappy-haired trouble makers; judgement time for those devilish, mischievous brats who had made his life a misery and caused him to lose his hair prematurely.

He took another look around him and saw that the room was filled with all those who had played truant when he had set the project only to return a few days later expecting him to believe that 'their grandmother had just died' or 'their house caught fire in the middle of the night'. Darren James was different from the rest, though. He was a law unto himself and had the infuriating habit of spending a whole lesson dreaming up ways in which to distract the rest of the class.

Darren had taken his seat at the back of

the classroom, biting his nails nervously. He didn't care that the few lines of his geography project were screwed up in a ball on his bedroom floor; he was thinking only of the fire extinguishers and how he would get away to set them off. The more he thought about the impending task, the quicker he shifted his position in his seat. His stomach tightened into a painful knot. The Toupee was straightening his tie and from where he sat Darren could see that there was a stain on it. He couldn't be sure what mood Mr Jones was in, but he did know that if he didn't get himself excused from the lesson as soon as possible he would surely wear out the seat of his pants from all the moving around he was doing. He couldn't wait any longer. This was it. Darren's hand shot up.

"Yes, James, what is it?" The Toupee asked, looking up from hooded eyes.

"Please sir," Darren pleaded, "I've got to go to the toilet."

The Toupee looked at Darren suspiciously and started to shake his head from side to side. He considered refusing James permission to leave the class, but what if he really did need to use the little boys' room? He could see Darren waving his arms wildly in the air shifting nervously in his chair with what looked like a pained expression on his face.

"I can never understand you kids," Mr Jones said. He had learnt over the years to stop his toupee from sliding when he spoke by tilting his head at a slight angle. It was this sight that always sent the pupils into raptures. To them he gave a good impression of the leaning tower of Pisa.

"You have just had a twenty minute break which should have given you adequate opportunity to visit the lavatory two or even three times," Mr Jones continued, letting out a sigh of resignation.

"But, Sir," begged Darren, "I'm really desperate."

"Go on," Mr Jones said, waving his arms in the general direction of the door. "But no loitering in the corridors."

"Thanks Sir." And with that Darren ran towards the front of the class and out into the corridor. "Yes!" he shouted, punching the air as he made his way up to the first floor, taking the steps two at a time. When he climbed the final step, he turned left and walked the few yards to where the fire point was situated. Stationing himself by the fire extinguishers outside the technology room, he looked about him furtively. There were a couple of girls from Year 12 walking towards their common room. Darren waited until they had turned the corner, counted to ten, then he pulled the metal container from its post and opened its cap.

There was a loud hiss. The foam started to spray everywhere. Darren was so surprised by the force at which the foam gushed out that he nearly slipped on the floor. Hurriedly, he placed the extinguisher on the floor, taking care to tread carefully through the puddle that had begun to form along the narrow hallway. He ran along the corridor letting off the other three as he went. Darren even laughed heartily as he began to enjoy his daring stunt. He wondered why he had been so nervous beforehand; this was not only easy, it was fun.

By the time he reached the end of the hall-way he was really out of breath. He took a breather as he made his way down to the ground floor. There was no one about and he had achieved his task so easily that he ambled along the hallway and even went as far as to let an extinguisher off in the boys' toilets. He was finished now. He turned the final corner and made his way down the stairs, avoiding any prying eyes as he did so. Outside the classroom, he straightened his tie and knocked on the door before he entered.

"Darren James!" The Toupee bellowed, "You took your time."

"Yes Sir, sorry Sir," Darren said in his calmest voice. "It must have been something I ate at breakfast; it didn't agree with my stomach."

When he heard a few of the class sniggering, Darren turned to face them with out-stretched arms, taking a bow at his audience.

Someone at the back farted, 'Prrp', as though joining in the ovation. "Urrgh!"

screamed a few girls as they held their noses between thumb and forefinger.

"Okay, Darren, go and sit down. I don't expect you have much more to do on your project," said Mr Jones, sarcastically, "but please will you get on with what is left. And try not to disturb the others."

Darren skulked back to his desk. He took out a fresh piece of paper from his pad and started to write, trying to remember the words he had left screwed up on his bedroom floor. But he didn't really care about the project. The Toupee would be angry when he saw it, but what was one more detention to a future member of the Smokers' Corner Crew? He'd easily completed the first of his SCC tasks and so everything was going to be all right.

While all this was going on, Tyrone was working in the computer room with Tenisha Markham and Anton Powell. The three of them had already completed their projects so The Toupee had given them the opportunity to do whatever they wanted. Tyrone, Tenisha and Anton had elected to work on the Year 8 magazine, and Tyrone was only sad that Darren wasn't with them. He knew what the reason was: the SCC. But Darren didn't seem to care any more and wasn't likely to take any advice he might be given. Tyrone only hoped that Darren would come back to his senses soon.

"Some of this stuff is brill," Tyrone said in amazement. "I mean I never knew any of this."

Anton looked up from the computer console that he had been working on. He walked over to where Tyrone was standing with a book in his hand.

"What's that Ty?" he asked.

"Well, all this historical business I've uncovered in this book. It's called 'African American Firsts', by Joan Potter and Constance Claytor."

Tenisha, who was busy sketching on her notepad, put her pencil in her mouth and looked at Tyrone, puzzled. Since Tyrone had voted himself in as editor and senior researcher for the magazine, she had seen his personality change. He had slowly transformed from the considerate person who would always listen to her complaints, her little white lies even, into a bullish slave driver. He had got really cross that morning when she'd arrived without any drawings for the magazine, and then became quite insulting when she explained that the dog had eaten them in the middle of the night.

The trouble with Tenisha's lies was that she often forgot to think them through. The words just came tumbling out before she had time to stop them. If only she had waited just a moment before blurting out her excuse, she would have remembered that Tyrone lived in the same street as her, just a few doors down on the other side of the road. He knew very well that Tenisha's family didn't have a dog, and so he also knew that was lying.

Well, what did he expect? she thought to herself as she chewed her pencil. She hadn't wanted to be Chief Artist in the first place, and she'd told him so. Everybody knew that she was hopeless at drawing. She wanted Anton's job, designing the cover and layout of the articles on the computer.

"What's so important about a few old fuddy duddies?" asked Anton.

"Don't you see?" Tyrone said exasperated. "All this info we've gathered, I'm sure not even Mr Robertson knows about."

"Of course he does," said Tenisha, removing her spectacles the way she always did when she needed time to think. She inspected them owlishly before cleaning them on her sleeve.

"Well," Tyrone queried, "if he has, why haven't we been told then?"

"I don't know, do I?" answered Tenisha. There goes Tyrone again, she thought inwardly. How was she to know what went on in the minds of teachers?

"Take this for instance," continued Tyrone, flicking through the pages of 'African American Firsts'. "The original electric light bulb was invented by a guy called Lewis Howard Latimer."

"Yes, so what?" Anton interjected.

"Do you know where he was from?" asked Tyrone.

Anton shrugged his shoulders. "America,

I guess."

"Yes America," stated Tyrone with a flourish. "But, more importantly, he was African-American!"

Tyrone sat down by one of the computer screens on a swivel chair and placed the book onto the desk. He placed his hands behind his head and swivelled around a full three hundred and sixty degrees, happy with his discovery.

The way Tyrone sat and the way he looked so pleased with himself reminded Tenisha of her father giving one of his lectures on not staying out late.

It was at this moment that they heard the fire bell ringing. The three would-be journalists jumped up with a start.

"I wonder what's going on?" Anton asked, frowning.

"It's most likely one of those fire drills that we've been having lately," Tenisha said with a shrug of her shoulders, and the three trudged out of the computer room.

The corridor was already full of pupils lining up against the walls according to their forms. Class 10C was going down the stairs as Tyrone closed the door to the computer room, Mr Singh walking down behind them. There were some boys half-way down the stairs jostling one another.

"In an orderly fashion now, remember the fire drills we've had!" Mr Singh shouted angrily.

Tyrone's eyes shifted around him before he pulled Tenisha by the arm towards him.

"We had better go into the playground to find Miss Bird," he said, remembering from previous drills that you had to find your form tutor.

Tenisha stared blankly at Tyrone; she was getting increasingly nervous. "Perhaps it's not a fire drill after all," she said biting her top lip. "Imagine if it's a real fire."

Tyrone did not answer: he was too preoccupied with making his way down the stairs.

In the playground, the teachers were frantically trying to get all the pupils into straight lines. They had their registers out and were ticking the names off of the pupils they could see. They tried desperately to get the pupils who were milling around in some kind of order.

Tyrone looked over at his form line and saw Darren standing towards the back of it. He made his way over to his friend.

"This is really good, isn't it?" Darren said in an unconvincing tone. He looked nervously over his shoulder, unsure of whether the two Year 12 girls had seen him in the corridor earlier, or whether The Toupee would suspect him of anything. He wiped his clammy hands on his trousers and hopped from one foot to the other. He could really use the toilet now.

Tyrone eyed Darren suspiciously. As far as he was concerned, standing around on a cold day doing nothing in the playground, when he could be upstairs finishing the magazine, wasn't much fun. And anyway, why was Darren dancing around in that manner, crossing and uncrossing his legs? Maybe it was a new dance that he had learnt from the SCC. Tyrone was pondering on this when he heard a shrill whistle coming from the other side of the playground. He turned in time to see Marvin, Roland and the rest of the Smokers' Corner Crew giving Darren the thumbs up signal.

Darren gave a little wave back. Seeing Marvin and the rest didn't make him feel quite so bad. Now that he had completed the first task, he was almost a member of the most exclusive club in school. Anyway, those Year 12 girls couldn't have seen him, he had made sure of that hadn't he? He only had a couple more tasks to do now.

Tyrone suddenly remembered what Patrick Annette had said at lunch time the day before.

"Do you know that Desmond Walker has been suspended for going into the girls' changing rooms?" he asked Darren excitedly.

Darren looked at him from the corner of his eye. "Yeah, and the girl in question is Aalisha Bennett," he said triumphantly.

"Oh."

"I don't know where you get your information," continued Darren in a superior voice, "but if that's the sort of stuff you're going to put in your stupid magazine, forget it."

"I just thought that maybe you hadn't heard," Tyrone stammered.

"Well you thought wrong then, didn't you? There are certain people in this school that get all the news first," said Darren looking over at Marvin.

Yes, I know, thought Tyrone inwardly. He was still feeling upset at the way Darren had talked to him, when Mr Singh came along to tell The Toupee that it had been a false alarm. All the pupils were now to be led back into the school.

The headmaster, Mr Fredricks, was very angry when he found out about the fire extinguishers and called an assembly of the whole school. He spoke about how the culprits were cowardly and despicable. He said that if any of the pupils knew who was involved, it was their duty to report it.

Tyrone didn't know what to do. He suspected that the Smokers' Corner Crew had something to do with the incident, and the way Darren was acting convinced him that his friend was not totally blameless. But what was he to do? He couldn't squeal on Darren. He was his best friend.

CHAPTER SIX

"So do you want to be in the SCC or not?" Marvin Johnson stood with his arms crossed as he looked at Darren.

It was a week since the incident with the fire extinguishers and the compliments of "well done" and "what a laugh" from the Smokers' Corner Crew had worn thin. They were now impatient to see some more action.

"Because if you want to pull out, you

can," continued Marvin.

It was Saturday morning and Darren was out shopping with his mother. The streets were crowded and he didn't want to be with her, let alone talk to Marvin who he had bumped into on the High Street. He stared hard at Marvin.

"I do want to be in the crew, but you know how hard it is to get teachers to leave their keys lying around."

Marvin shook his head and kissed his teeth. He gazed lovingly at his reflection in a shop window, liking what he saw. He was wearing black Karl Kani baggy trousers, white designer trainers with the air bubble, and his black hooded Oakland Raiders jacket. He'd only bought the jacket the week before and it had cost him a lot of money. As he adjusted his jacket he wondered how he was going to get those weedy kids in Year 7 and 8 to give him some extra cash for parking their bikes. He had to make some more easy money so that he could buy the CD he had seen earlier.

Marvin took out his Gianni Versace sunglasses from the inside pocket of his jacket and put them on. He took a final look at his reflection before turning back to Darren.

"You know what they say? He who dares, wins."

Yes, thought Darren to himself, they should also say that he who dares usually gets into trouble. He shifted his feet nervously as his mother came out of the butcher's shop.

"Darren," Yvonne said, giving Marvin the once over, "put this in the carrier bag." She took another look at the older boy who was standing by her son. He seemed to signal trouble. She asked herself where he could possibly have found the money to buy such exclusive garments. But what worried her most was the whiff of tobacco that came from his clothes. Why would Darren want to keep company with an obvious layabout like this? She took her son by the arm and pulled him towards her as she made her way along the street.

Embarrassed, Darren pulled himself away from his mother's grip. "Look, I'll see what I can do," he told Marvin.

Marvin smiled and the two boys touched fists. Darren watched him walk away and then ran after his mother.

Yvonne, fashionably attired in a short A-line skirt, high heels and a red beret, was very popular. Every so often, as they made their way along the High Street, she would bump into one of her friends and they would start talking for what seemed to her son like forever. It was the same every Saturday morning and Darren hated it. He'd have to get out of their weekly shopping trips when he became a member of the SCC.

Old Mrs Braithwaite pointed at him. "Hasn't he grown?!" she cried.

"Yes," replied Yvonne in a smug fashion. "I think it's all the junk food the youngsters eat these days."

Darren knew why his mother wanted him with her on Saturday mornings. It was so she could show him off like one of those sideshow freaks at the funfair. He squirmed as he looked over at Mrs Braithwaite's hairy chin. She was every young boy's nightmare, the kind of woman you prayed would never insist on kissing you. And she made the same comment every week about how tall he had grown.

"Darren," Yvonne said once they'd passed Mrs Braithwaite, "does that boy you were talking to earlier take drugs?"

His mother's words were like a bullet in the head for Darren. Why would she say such a thing? As far as he could tell Marvin and the rest would never do such things.

"No, Mum...of course not."

"It's just the way he looked," Yvonne said in a concerned way. "All dopey, looking really foolish."

Darren tried to avoid his mother's stare by walking quickly towards the next shop and staring absent-mindedly inside.

"Do you know what I'm talking about?"

"Yes, Mum," Darren answered swiftly.

Yvonne decided not to press the issue but to wait until Darren's father arrived home that evening. She'd get him to have a word with his son.

Darren was happy when his mother abandoned the conversation, as he was in no mood for small talk. His mind was set on the second task: how was he going to get Mr Henry's key? What was the price of failure? He dreaded to think of the answer to that one.

When his mother stopped outside the greengrocers, the answer came to him like a bolt of lightning. Right out of the blue. The more he thought about it, the more he was convinced that it would work. He knew he would have to treat Tyrone better for the next few days if the plan was going to work, but that would be easy. He knew Tyrone was jealous of him.

I bet he also wants to be a member, he thought inwardly. He shook the thought swiftly from his mind. "No," he said to himself, "that's taking it a little too far." Tyrone was a teacher's pet, a mummy's boy and as far as Darren was concerned, Tyrone just wasn't cool. He was always making sure he got to school on time. In fact, if Darren thought about it, he couldn't remember a single time when Tyrone had been late for school. Marvin and the rest of the crew, on the other hand, were always late.

No, Tyrone was only good to ask favours from. Just last week he had asked Remi out for Darren. But Remi had made some comment about the way Darren's clothes smelled now and if he stopped smoking she'd consider it. What a cheek! His clothes didn't smell any different. In fact, since he started to smoke, he couldn't smell anything at all, apart from the breath of the guys in the SCC. But that hadn't been Tyrone's fault. He'd kept his side of the bargain and talked to Remi, as Darren had asked him. Darren thought Tyrone would be good for another favour too; one that would help him with SCC task number two.

At least he would if Darren made like they were spars again.

While Darren was preparing his plan, Tyrone was at home helping his mother with the washing up. He enjoyed helping her with things around the house, even more so since she'd been looking more tired. He had seen her come back from a hard day's work many times and immediately start slaving over the stove in the kitchen and then, just as she was about to sit down, Aaron would start to cry. He'd seen the strain on his mum's face as she'd get up to see to him and he secretly wished that he was old enough to make enough money to take his mother on a cruise around the world. A big ship like the Titanic would do, without the iceberg of course.

"Mum," Tyrone said in his most serious voice.

Marcia looked up from her chores and took off her yellow rubber gloves. The look on her son's face and the sound of his voice meant that there was something on his mind. She may not have had a lot of time to spend with her kids but when they had a problem she would go out of her way to sort it out.

"If you suspected something bad of a friend," Tyrone looked hard into his mother's eyes, "would you snitch?"

Marcia Miller thought about the question for a brief moment before replying.

"Sometimes people have to do things which may often not be popular at the time, but in the long run it often turns out for the best."

Tyrone concentrated on his mother's words.

"But what if it gets in the way of your friendship? Would you still snitch?" he asked, a little more determinedly.

Marcia frowned. "Is there something you're not telling me?"

"No, Mum," Tyrone replied hurriedly. "I've just remembered that I have to go to the library." He headed for the door. His mother was getting a little too close for comfort and he didn't want to tell her about what he suspected Darren of doing. Anyway, it wasn't as if he knew for sure that Darren had let off the fire extinguishers at school.

"Tyrone, the rest of the plates...!" his mother called after him, but it was too late. Tyrone was already out the front door and trudging down the road.

All he could think about was the way his friend had dumped him. As far as Tyrone was concerned Darren really had a bad attitude these days.

As he walked up the road he remembered the game he and Darren used to play where they would walk along the pavement taking care not to stand on the cracks. If you stepped on one it meant that you were doomed to a day of bad luck. Thinking of the way Darren had changed, Tyrone had no intention of playing it today.

As he passed the Johnson's house at the end of the street, Sabre, their Jack Russell terrier, charged out from behind a hedge yelping and snarling.

"Damn!" cried Tyrone as he made to run away. He hadn't seen this dog for ages, ever since he had a paper round last year in fact. He knew the dog very well. Tyrone had lost count of the times that he had walked up the Johnson's garden path with a bag laden with newspapers and, as if from nowhere, Sabre would appear, trapping him between the front door and the gate to the street. He would then have to make his escape by jumping the fence that separated the Johnsons' house from their neighbour's. He had even had to abandon his newspaper bag once and make his exit by leaping over the flower bed and running through the hedge. He had scratched his arms and his face that time, but he'd ignored the pain because Sabre was right behind him barking for all he was worth.

Tyrone had run to Mr Patel's shop faster than an Olympic gold medallist, but the shopkeeper hadn't seen the funny side of it. He'd been cheesed off when Tyrone told him that he had been unable to deliver the newspapers and he'd given Tyrone the sack on the spot.

Now, confronted as he was by Sabre again, the fear that he felt back then returned. Panicking, Tyrone turned to run in the opposite direction, and found himself running straight into Darren.

"What's with the rush?" Darren asked in a sharp voice as he straightened himself up.

Tyrone was surprised to see Darren on his road; it had been ages since he had telephoned or come round. "Oh, nothing," he said, eyeing Sabre nervously from the corner of his eye.

Darren playfully slapped Tyrone on the back of the neck. "What's up with you? Can't I come to see my best friend sometime?" he asked.

Tyrone felt better when he heard this. Maybe Darren was his old self again. Maybe, but maybe not.

"Yes," Tyrone began, "but I don't see much of you these days. I've even tried to phone but you weren't in."

Darren guiltily turned his head away from Tyrone's icy stare. "Yeah, I know," he said. "Something came up."

Tyrone spun around. "That's what I mean...something is always coming up lately."

By this time Sabre, having escaped the confines of his garden and revelling in his new-found freedom, had started to snap at Darren's trousers. Darren picked up a stone from the side of the pavement and aimed it at the Jack Russell. The stone hit the dog soundly on the rump. With a yelp, it staggered back and then ran up the road in terror.

Darren changed the direction of the conversation. If Tyrone laboured on the breakdown of their friendship he might not be able to use him for what he wanted.

"Where were you going?"

"To the library."

"To the library!" Darren exclaimed incredulously.

"Yeah, what's wrong with that?"

"Nothing," said Darren with a smirk. "I just thought that we could do something together, like the old times."

The old times, mused Tyrone to himself. Darren and he used to do so much together. He remembered the time when they had gone to the woods last summer. They had somehow lost each other and he'd been a little frightened when he'd realised that he was suddenly alone. He'd felt the same as when he'd watched an old Dracula movie late one night. He had called out for Darren but there was no answer. Then, just as he was about to turn round and head back home, Darren had jumped out of the bushes waving his arms about and scaring him out of his wits. Darren had laughed so much he had tears running down his face.

That had been a wonderful summer, they had done so much together: rollerblading in the park, minigolf every Wednesday in the park by Darren's, and they had made a tree house in the woods which they named The Den. Not a very original name, but it was theirs, a place they would go every Friday. But since Darren had become friends with Marvin, he had not even mentioned The Den, let alone want to go there.

As he thought about going off with Darren, Tyrone remembered the magazine. He really should finish it off, but it might not be such a bad idea to do something with Darren for a change.

"Okay," he declared. "What did you have in mind?"

Darren shrugged his shoulders absentmindedly. "I don't know, perhaps we can take in a movie or go bowling."

"But I haven't got much money," said Tyrone.

"Don't worry, I'll sort you out," replied Darren. He was used to paying for his friend and, anyway, if his plan was going to work he'd have to keep Tyrone sweet.

Tyrone happily agreed. After all, bowling was one of the few games he regularly beat Darren at.

"All right, Darren, and I can fill you in on all the gossip."

"If you must," said Darren, a bored look on his face.

The bowling alley that they went to was a popular one for most of the kids in the area because you were able to go there and use its facilities without worrying about being picked on, no matter which school you went to.

There had been a truce called in the bowling alley for as long as anyone could remember, and the manager made sure that it remained in place. He had introduced special prices for school children at certain times of the day. The pupils of Drummond Hill loved going there, especially on days when the youth centre was closed, and particularly when they were only charged half price. Today was such a day and, as usual, the alley was packed. All the players were dressed in the regulation bowling shoes and shirts and the music blared from the loudspeakers. It was one of those old rock and roll songs, Rock Around the Clock.

Darren sauntered up to the counter and paid the lady.

"You're lucky, there's a lane free," she shouted above the loud music. She blew a big bubble from the gum that she was chewing as she handed Darren two tickets.

Tyrone was over by the drinks counter. He ordered two Cokes and took them over to the lane Darren had booked. As Tyrone slipped on his bowling shoes, Darren made him laugh with an impression of Elvis Presley, gyrating his hips wildly to the music.

"Hold on a minute," said Darren as he stopped in the middle of his dance routine.

Tyrone, bowling ball in hand, looked up at Darren.

"What's the matter?" he asked, in a concerned voice.

"There's Marvin and the crew," said Darren pointing to the far end of the hall.

Tyrone followed Darren's hand with his eyes. He could see Marvin, Roland and the rest standing up, arguing among themselves. They were pointing at two boys standing alone, waiting for the SCC to finish their game.

"I wonder what's going on," said Darren, a frown on his face.

The music from the loudspeakers was still blaring but that didn't stop Marvin and his boys attracting a lot of attention from all the commotion they were making. Everyone seemed to have stopped their game to see what was going on.

"I should find out what's happening," continued Darren. He went towards his new friends.

"Why do you need to see them?" asked Tyrone, who felt suddenly insecure. "I thought you wanted to be with me."

Darren stopped in his tracks. He needed Tyrone for his plan, it was true. But Tyrone would come through whatever, he was sure of that. Marvin could not be left waiting.

"Sorry Ty," said Darren, simply. "They need me over there."

Tyrone sighed heavily as he put his bowling ball down and sauntered after Darren.

They reached the lane in time to hear Marvin say to his boys, "I like that jacket."

He was pointing at the younger of the two boys. The boy had on a black bomber jacket with Chicago Bulls sewn on the back. Marvin strolled across to where the two boys were, while his buddies waited.

"Hey, I like your jacket," Marvin said gruffly. "How about letting me try it on?"

The boy, younger and smaller than Marvin, hesitated. But when Marvin, thumbs in pockets, feet apart, pelvis forward, stepped closer, the boy slipped off the jacket and handed it over. Marvin's friends lounged against a wall, watching.

"Looks good," Marvin said, and he shouted to his pals, "Not bad, huh?" They gave their approval.

"Hey," Marvin said to the boy, "I'll keep

it." He started to walk off.

The boy came after him and jumped on his back. Marvin threw him off, turned and slapped his face. His three SCC mates came running up to help. The boy panicked when he saw that he was outnumbered and ran off, his friend close behind him.

Tyrone's jaw almost hit the floor when he saw what had happened. He looked at Darren.

"That's well out of order," he said.

Darren couldn't move, it was as though his feet were stuck to the floor.

"Yeah," he replied, "but he must have done something to deserve it."

Tyrone was shocked by what Darren was saying. It was obvious to anyone with half a brain cell that Marvin had acted as though he were Mike Tyson or something. He took a look around him; everyone had returned to their game as though nothing had happened. That was the problem: all the kids at Drummond Hill let Marvin and his gang get away with anything and nobody ever tried to stop them.

105

Feeling angry, Tyrone headed back to continue his game. He glanced back to see if Darren was behind, but realised that he was not following. Darren was standing with the SCC, laughing and admiring the new jacket that Marvin had acquired.

"I'll see you tomorrow," Darren said when he saw Tyrone's accusing face.

What a liberty, thought Tyrone. He just dumps me in favour of them. I'll show him.

And with that he walked out of the bowling alley.

CHAPTER SEVEN

A week later, lying on his bed, Tyrone was thinking about how much Darren had changed. He couldn't understand what was going on and felt as though Darren had taken off and was leaving him far behind. He hadn't phoned or come round for several days, and they had previously always gone everywhere together! As far as he was concerned, Darren seemed to be taking him for granted. Like the day after the incident with the fire extinguishers, when Darren had begged him to ask Remi out for him. He hadn't had the guts to do it himself. And even though Tyrone knew Remi liked Darren she had refused to go out with him unless he stopped smoking and left the SCC crew. It seemed that everyone in their year knew about Darren's smoking.

Tyrone thought he knew what to do. He stood up and went to his dressing room table and opened a drawer. Inside were the hair clippers he and Darren used to style their hair. As he took out the clippers, he thought pensively about the new designs that he and Darren had sculpted on each other's heads. He remembered the time when the high top style had been all the rage at school and they had both decided that the look would suit them just fine.

Everything had started off all right and Tyrone had given Darren a nice shape to his haircut. But when it came to his turn, Darren had got carried away with the music that was playing on the radio and hadn't realised how much of Tyrone's hair he was cutting away.

When Patricia had come into the room and started laughing uncontrollably, a vexed Tyrone had ordered Darren to do something about it. Darren did do something. He gave him the shortest high top in town. It had been so embarrassing and he'd had to endure the endless comments at school like, "Who cuts your hair?" and "Did you have an argument with your lawnmower?" and stuff. But that was okay, because Darren went and cut his in a similar fashion out of solidarity with his best friend.

That was how close he and Darren had been. They identified with each other, and the best way to do that was to be seen looking the same.

Now, standing in front of the mirror, clippers in hand, Tyrone didn't care any more. He didn't want to look like Darren any longer. He switched on the clippers and they hummed gently as he shaved the side of his hair. It was a style that he had admired for a long time, but he knew that Darren hated. That didn't bother him any longer. If Darren wanted to carry on acting like an idiot, he was going to try his best not to look like him.

Once he'd finished Tyrone stood back, nodding at his reflection a final time in the mirror. He looked good. He felt free.

When he made his way down the stairs, his mother was just coming in through the front door laden down with shopping.

"Mmm," she said admiringly, "you look very smart, Tyrone. You must wear your hair like that more often."

Tyrone smiled, happy that his mother approved. "Perhaps I will," he said.

"Are you going to the youth centre tonight?" asked Marcia as she put her heavy shopping bags down on the floor.

"Yeah, I was just on my way out," Tyrone said, squeezing into his puffa jacket.

"Try not to be too late when you come back," said Marcia sitting down. Her large hazel eyes set in an attractive oval face hid the effect of years of menial work. She took off her shoes and rubbed her tired feet. Her

110

hands, rough from the many floors they had cleaned, massaged her aching limbs.

Marcia smoothed her hands on her jeans before standing. At school she had always been the tallest girl in her class, 5 feet 9 inches, with the solid muscle of a keen sportswoman from training as a netball player. In her youth she had been self-conscious of her frizzy hair and had experimented with permanent waves and various colour dyes. Now she chose to wear one of many wigs, exposing her hair only at night when no one was around to see. She had grown into her distinctive facial features: dimpled cheeks, like her son's, high cheekbones and full lips.

She turned to her oldest son and smiled to herself. He reminded her of his father. She took him to her and hugged him tightly, kissing him lightly on the forehead.

"Watch my hair, Mum!" said Tyrone, embarrassed.

The youth centre that Tyrone and the rest of his friends went to was where many children in the area went to have fun. Crisps, sweets, chips, drinks and games were supplied by the two supervisors and the music was anything that the kids themselves wanted — usually reggae, swing beat, and, if you were really sad, rock 'n' roll. The music was normally supplied by the more hip kids. Patricia usually brought her own.

The kids had organised most of the games that took place in the evenings, like table tennis, snooker, Twister, computer games and five-a-side football, and even the occasional talent competition. The football and the Wednesday night basketball were played enthusiastically at the far end of the big hall. There were a few tables and chairs placed along the side of one of the walls so the children could sit down, talk and eat.

Tyrone, like all the kids who frequented the club, liked coming to the youth centre because there were no teachers, no stress and definitely no homework.

Throughout the evening people kept coming up to Tyrone and commenting on how great his new haircut looked. Robert Collins even said something about how he could now tell the difference between him and Darren. It was true, Darren and he had been best friends for so long that they even dressed similarly. It felt good to have his own identity.

Even Remi seemed impressed. "You look like the Fresh Prince of Bel Air," she said. "I'm sure that all the girls are going to fancy you."

As if! thought Tyrone to himself.

He looked about him to see who else was around and noticed Patricia dancing to the music. Tyrone walked over to her.

"What do you think?" he asked as he pointed to his hair.

Patricia looked at him as though he was last night's dinner and she sniffed the air with disdain. "Big deal!" she said as her lips curled up at the sides in a sly leer.

Tyrone stood frozen to the spot. He knew that Patricia didn't particularly care for him, but he quite liked her and he didn't think that her attitude towards him was fair, especially since he'd never said a bad word to her. Tyrone opened his mouth to speak but another quick look at the dancing girl's face showed him that he would most likely get thumped if he disturbed her.

From the corner of his eye he saw Darren standing with two boys over by the football pitch. Tyrone cheered up a little as he made his way over.

As he approached, Darren noticed him and immediately fell about laughing uncontrollably and pointing.

"See what hanging around geeks like Anton and Tenisha does to you?"

Tyrone wanted to hit out at Darren. But before he could react, one of the boys, who Tyrone didn't really know, shook his head. "Leave it out," the boy said to Darren. He turned to face Tyrone and offered him his fist in greeting. They touched. "We need an extra player for the five-a-side football match tonight. Do you fancy playing?" he asked.

Tyrone's heart raced. He had never played for any of the youth centre's teams before. Perhaps this would take his mind off Darren's taunts.

"Yeah, all right," he answered swiftly.

Tyrone found it hard to sleep that night and Darren's behaviour was partly to blame. His friend's ever-changing attitude towards him was confusing and Tyrone didn't even know whether they were still friends. He'd have to deal with that as and when the time came.

But apart from the confusion over his friend, Tyrone was still on a buzz from the five-a-side football. That had been great. He had won the match for the team by the touch of quality that he'd brought with him. But despite all the composure that Tyrone had showed, the team was not able to capitalise on it until the last minute of the game when Tyrone had decided to move upfield.

Darren had taken a corner over on the left wing and slid it deftly to Nipper Reid, the team's tiny midfield general. Nipper back-heeled the ball to where Tyrone was waiting patiently. With a swivel of his hips, Tyrone nutmegged the opposing defender and rounded the goalkeeper who was flailing on the ground. A classic goal. The youth centre fans were delirious with joy; Tyrone had won the game for them.

When the game finished and he was carried on the shoulders of the team, Tyrone had felt on top of the world. Everyone had been pleased for him — even Darren — and Remi had come up to him and planted a wet kiss on his cheek. That had really made his day.

Now, as he lay on his bed, Tyrone smiled contentedly as he closed his eyes for the night. Before he fell asleep he promised himself that he would not wash his face for a month.

The next morning, on his way to school, Nipper Reid came running up to Tyrone. His face was screwed up in a frown and he looked as if he had lost a pound and found a penny.

"What did you think about my performance last night?" Tyrone said, trying to make conversation.

"Okay, I guess," replied Nipper.

The boys continued towards the bus stop in silence. Tyrone could feel that Nipper had something on his mind.

"What's up?" asked Tyrone after a brief pause.

116

"I don't know how to tell you," Nipper said.

"Tell me what?" said Tyrone, suddenly starting to feel worried.

"Well...it's just..." Nipper began.

"What is it?"

"Well, Darren is your friend and all. So I guess I can tell you."

Tyrone leaned closer. Despite what had gone on between him and Darren, if he had a problem then he was prepared to help if he could.

"Last night after the match..."

"Yeah?"

"Darren and the SCC, the police, the noise, oh..."

Tyrone spun around. "Stop blabbering," he said grabbing his small friend by the collar. "Get to the point, man!"

Nipper went on to explain how he had seen Darren making his way out of the youth centre with Marvin and the other members of the SCC. They had been walking along the street, joking and shouting.

"I couldn't catch everything that was going on, mind," said Nipper.

Tyrone wished Nipper would get on with it.

"Because I didn't want them to see me," added Nipper.

"Go on."

"There was this old lady. One moment she was walking along and then the next she starts shouting and hollering." Nipper was in a real state by this time and if Tyrone had not been so concerned about Darren he would have asked him to ease up.

"Then Marvin and the rest started running..." Nipper continued.

"What about Darren?" Tyrone asked in a concerned tone.

"He was running as well. Then the police came running and they started shoving and pushing and they had the SCC against the wall and all."

Nipper was talking so fast that he wasn't making very much sense to Tyrone. It took the dimunitive boy a while to make himself understood. From what Tyrone could gather, Darren had been very close to getting himself nicked by the police. What was going on? Tyrone couldn't figure it out.

CHAPTER EIGHT

"Hello Tyrone."

Tyrone turned to look. Remi Oluseyi was standing by her locker on the first floor landing.

"Oh, hi Remi," he said in an embarrassed tone. He still hadn't washed his face since the football match and had spent the last few nights dreamily thinking about her. In fact, every time he had seen her at school since, she had smiled at him.

There were some boys rushing about the hall playing football with a rolled up newspaper. One of them, in his haste to score, accidently pushed Remi into Tyrone. Tyrone caught her before she could hurt herself.

"Are you all right?" he asked, concerned.

"Yeah, sure," said Remi as she flashed him her most electrifying smile and flicked a wisp of hair from her eyes.

"I heard that you were editing the Year 8 magazine?"

Tyrone puffed out his chest importantly. He had become very well known among the pupils of the lower school since he'd started the magazine. Bending down, he picked Remi's bag from where it lay on the floor and handed it to her.

"Yeah, that's right," he said, shifting his feet uncomfortably.

"I was wondering…" Remi began, placing the bag under her arm, "if you needed another pair of hands?"

"Of course," said Tyrone excitedly. He was

happy that somebody else was showing an interest in the magazine. His requests for other helpers in Year 7 and 8 had been met with a lukewarm response. Also he was finding it increasingly difficult to monitor the work of his co-workers, Anton and Tenisha. He was forever having to chase them all over school to find out what they had done. Remi's offer to help would make life a little easier.

"There was something else I wanted to ask," said Remi, interrupting Tyrone's train of thought. She flashed him another one of her smiles.

"What's that?" asked Tyrone.

"That would be telling, wouldn't it?" said Remi mysteriously.

"So tell me," said Tyrone anxiously.

The bell sounded for the next lesson.

"Look, meet me here at lunch time and I'll fill you in," she said as she made her way to the form room.

"Okay."

Just as Tyrone turned towards the form room Darren came rushing along the corridor.

"Here you are!" he said breathlessly.

"What is it?" asked Tyrone.

"Meet me by the boys' toilets at lunch time," Darren said as he rushed off once more.

"No...but...are you okay? Look...I can't," said Tyrone stamping his feet in frustration. Darren was already out of sight before Tyrone could finish his sentence. He wanted to ask Darren a few questions about the night before.

Tyrone stamped his feet again. He had to let one of his friends down, but which one? He went into his form room trying to figure out what to do.

At lunch time, Tyrone was waiting by the boys' toilets. He was still upset that he had to let Remi down but even though Darren had been acting a bit weird lately, he was still his best friend. Best friends did come first, didn't they?

"Thanks for coming Ty," said Darren as soon as he saw Tyrone. "I appreciate it."

"What do you want?" Tyrone asked curtly.

"I need your help," said Darren shyly.

Tyrone became suspicious. He couldn't make out Darren's manner.

"Why, what's wrong?"

"Can I ask you a small favour?"

"Has it got anything to do with last night?" Tyrone asked frowning.

Darren shifted his feet uneasily but ignored Tyrone's question. He had wanted Tyrone to be sweeter than this. He needed this favour badly. "I want you to leave the music door open when you put all the instruments away this afternoon."

Tyrone was aghast at Darren's suggestion. "You know I can't do that!"

"Why not?"

"Because Mr Henry trusts me to lock up after, that's why not."

"So what, don't you trust me?"

"I can't," said Tyrone determinedly. He turned his face to avoid Darren's stare. Why did Darren want the door open, anyway? Why was it so important? Why had Darren avoided telling him what went on yesterday? These questions and more spun around in

Tyrone's head as he stared at the floor. He made to walk past his friend.

"Look, are you going to do it or not?" Darren said as he moved to block Tyrone's escape route. He had his arms folded across his chest in a menacing way.

Tyrone merely looked blankly back at him. Who did he think he was talking to? Darren now behaved like a paid-up member of the SCC, as if he owned the place, but Tyrone wasn't about to let himself be bullied into action.

Seeing that his hard-man tactics weren't working, Darren got down on one knee and clasped his hands together as though in prayer. "Please Tyrone," he begged. "I need the door open today."

"No," said Tyrone, making to push past. Then, changing his mind, he turned. "First tell me about what went on yesterday after the youth centre closed."

Darren's face suddenly changed. "All right then," he said, so angry he almost foamed at the mouth. "If that's the way you want it, I'm terminating our friendship as from now."

Tyrone didn't like what he was hearing and if there was one thing that he wanted, it was to remain best friends with Darren. "Okay, I'll do it," he said quickly, "but only this once."

Darren jumped up and down with joy. "Tyrone, man, I could kiss you."

"If you did that, I'd definitely not help you."

"Laters," said Darren winking as he walked away.

When Darren was gone Tyrone stood and thought about what had gone on between them. He knew that Mr Henry would be livid if he found out. He could even be expelled. But his friendship was proving to be something he just couldn't walk away from. How could he let Darren down if he was in a fix?

Darren walked into his form room much relieved that he had been able to get Tyrone to do as he asked. For a while there, he didn't think he'd agree.

Things hadn't been going smoothly as far as Marvin and the SCC were concerned. Things had started to change when he had seen what went on last night. They had been walking home together and sharing a joke among themselves. Darren hadn't actually seen what went on, all he'd heard was the old lady shouting.

"Dem rob me purse!" she hollered in a strong Jamaican patois.

Darren had been frozen to the spot as Marvin and Roland sprinted up the High Street. He had looked about him, wondering what was going on when the old lady gave lie to her frail appearance and set about whacking Steven on the back of the head with the umbrella that she carried with her.

"Arrgh!" Steven had shrieked as he cowered in a doorway with his arms protecting his head.

But the old lady was in full flow, giving Steven a kick below the knee with her Hush Puppie boots.

"Okay!" Steven bellowed, as the pain triggered off the tears he had been holding back.

Darren had suddenly been shaken into life with a start as he heard the police sirens wailing all around. There was a real commotion. Before Darren could say 'Jack Robinson' he found himself with his hands pinned up behind so that they hurt, and his face jammed up against the glass front of the shop. He moved his head to one side, straining to see who had slammed him so hard in the back. He heard the crackle of the police radio as he stared up into the growling face of the uniformed officer. Darren opened his mouth to speak.

"What's going on?" he stammered, wincing from the pain in his arms.

The police officer answered by tightening his grip. Darren screamed.

"Nooo…!"

From the corner of his eye Darren could see Marvin and Roland being marched back by two burly policemen. The old lady was squinting hard at them.

"It's dem," she cried as she hit Marvin a resounding clap around the back of the neck with her umbrella.

Marvin scowled at the lady, but didn't flinch an inch from the blow he had received.

"What about this one?" asked the policeman as he held Darren's hands tightly.

"No, he's not one of them."

Darren felt sweet relief as the pain in his arm was relaxed.

"You, get lost!" the officer ordered, giving Darren a shove.

Darren didn't need telling twice. Without turning he trotted up the road and kept on going until he arrived home. He had never been so glad to reach the sanctuary of his yard before. He didn't even bother to brush his teeth, but crashed into his bed fully clothed, sobbing silently to himself.

All that afternoon Tyrone couldn't concentrate on his work. Even through history, his favourite lesson. All that had been on his mind was the favour that Darren had asked him to carry out. He would have liked to go home straight away, but he knew he couldn't

128

do that. He was still preoccupied with this problem when he felt someone nudging him in the ribs.

It was Anton, who was seated next to him and was trying to warn him. But it was too late.

"Tyrone!" shouted Mr Robertson from the front of the class. "You won't find the answer looking out of the window."

Tyrone, startled, sat up. "Wha...? Wha...what do you mean, Sir?" he managed to blurt out.

"Can you really not tell me any more about the conspirators involved in the Gunpowder Plot?" Mr Robertson asked, looking straight at him. He was quite surprised to find Tyrone inattentive during his lesson. That was not usually the case. Tyrone was one of the brightest students in his year.

A few of the class laughed nervously at Tyrone's obvious discomfort. Mr Robertson turned to face them.

"No talking over there!" he snapped.

"They were a group of Catholics led by Robert Catesby and they plotted to blow up

Parliament in 1605 because the king kept passing all these laws against Catholics. It didn't work out because Guy Fawkes was caught before he could set off the gunpowder under the Parliament buildings," said Tyrone smugly, now that he had regained his composure.

Mr Robertson rolled his eyes towards the ceiling.

"Why didn't you say that in the first place?"

Tyrone wasn't about to tell him.

The music lesson later on that day was even worse. Tyrone was dreading being asked to put the instruments away. Mr Henry always asked him. That was the problem with teachers, they were too predictable at times.

Mr Henry modelled the presentation of his lessons on the BBC news. He relied heavily on alliteration. "Holst's Planet Suite...brings panic to the planets, it scares the solar system." The students would laugh when he used a barrage of metaphors. In his shaky voice he would describe something simple like singing harmonies as "the dawn chorus of nightingales".

Tyrone was still looking at Mr Henry when Remi came in late and after a mild rebuke from the teacher, sat down in an empty seat beside Patrick Annette. Tyrone was surprised. Why would Remi sit next to him? Patrick Annette was the sap of the class and was treated even worse than Anton. Like Anton, he had no sense of fashion. But at least Anton didn't gossip. Patrick didn't know the meaning of the word secret. Ugghh!! What was Remi playing at? There she was, the best-looking girl in their year, voluntarily sitting next to the grass of their year. How gross.

When the bell rang for the end of the lesson, Tyrone started to panic. He had been dreading this moment. All kinds of things kept going through his mind. Throughout the lesson he had wished that Mr Henry would change his usual routine, but that would have been like asking for a miracle.

"Tyrone, would you pack the instruments away?" asked Mr Henry, handing the keys to his most trusted pupil.

Tyrone's heart was thumping. He shook his head, he didn't want them.

"But...Sir," he pleaded.

"And do it quickly. You can return the keys to me in the staff room when you've finished."

Tyrone took the keys reluctantly from his teacher. The rest of the class had been dismissed and were making their way noisily out of the room.

Tyrone was still in two minds about whether or not to leave the door open for Darren. He knew he shouldn't, but the thought of losing his best friend outweighed the consequences of getting caught. And anyway, he could always claim that it was a mistake. After all, everyone made a mistake at some time, didn't they?

Tyrone put the instruments away and left the door of the room unlocked but closed. He took the keys to Mr Henry in the staff room.

"Thanks Tyrone, you're a real friend." Darren placed an arm around his friend's shoulder. He had been pleased when Tyrone had given him the chance to get one of the Year 10 mock exam papers from Mr Henry's room and now it was all over he was feeling much better than he had earlier. He had found the whole experience quite exciting and had felt a little like James Bond or an FBI agent taking top secret papers from the enemy.

Tyrone didn't feel the same elation as his friend. He had been put in a position of trust and had abused it.

"Tell me Darren," he asked, "what did you want the door left open for?"

Darren threw his arms wide open exaggeratedly, trying to show that he was shocked by Tyrone's question.

"What, don't you trust me?'

"No, it's not that," started Tyrone. "It's just that I think you're getting yourself mixed up in things that you can't handle."

"I can't believe you said that," said Darren, annoyed at Tyrone's comment.

133

"You're such a wimp at times."

Tyrone gritted his teeth in frustration. After all he had done for his friend, putting himself at risk like he did, and Darren wasn't even grateful. "Anyway," he said, "I've got the magazine to finish off."

"Yes, why don't you do that?" Darren teased. "Run along to Anton and Tenisha."

Tyrone watched Darren walk away. Everything seemed to be getting worse and there was nothing he could about it.

CHAPTER NINE

The whole of the Smokers' Corner Crew were at the amusement arcade. Roland and Daniel were standing against a wall, hands in pockets, staring aimlessly at the floor. A couple of others were sharing a cigarette near the entrance and Darryl Hall was, as usual, over by the fruit machines. Each of them, apart from Marvin, was wearing the same Oakland Raiders American football jackets, designer trainers and dark sunglasses. Marvin Johnson, who had been bothering two girls playing a computer game, looked up as Darren walked in.

Everyone except Darryl stopped what they were doing and gathered round. Marvin was dressed slightly differently from the others, wearing the black and white hooded jacket he had 'taxed' from the young boy at the bowling alley.

"So did you manage to get it?" asked Marvin.

Darren looked at him before answering. Standing there he realised that he had a lot of power. Just at that moment, he was the most important person in the arcade. Everyone's attention was on him. It crossed his mind for a second that he could hold an auction for the papers that he had in his pocket, but he thought better of it. He didn't want to fall out with the SCC now, when he was so close to being accepted.

"What happened last night?" asked Darren, in a concerned way.

"What do you care?" Marvin replied scornfully.

"Unhh?"

"We all saw you running with your tail between your legs," Steven chided. He had been ribbed by his friends earlier, on account of how the old lady had made him cry. He wasn't about to remind them of it, and picking on Darren was the best way he knew of deflecting criticism from himself.

"So what happened?" Darren asked again.

"They had to let us off when they found out we were too young to be charged," Marvin said, pushing out his chest importantly.

"Oh," muttered Darren to himself. Things still didn't make sense to him.

Marvin shoved Darren in the chest with the palm of his hand. "Let's have a look then," he demanded.

Darren sniffed the air, it smelled pungent. Steven was smoking a rolled cigarette and blew the smoke over Darren's face. Darren coughed, the smoke burning his throat and stinging his eyes as he breathed in.

"What's that?"

"Weed," replied Steven, offering Darren the spliff. "Do you want a drag?"

Steven's eyes were all bloodshot and half-closed. He seemed to have difficulty in standing straight and used his free hand to balance himself by holding on to one of the pinball machines. Darren shook his head.

"Go on, take a pull of it," Steven nudged.

Darren shook his head again. "Maybe later," he answered. He didn't want to give his new friends the impression that he was a baby or anything, he knew that the cigarette that he was being offered was a drug. He had heard about them, they had other names for it like 'chronic' and 'dope' and all sorts of other fancy names. He wasn't prepared to try it out just yet. His mother's warnings about the dangers of drugs, and how she would skin him alive if she ever caught him with any, rang in his head as he dug his hand in his pocket.

Darren scanned the room quickly and took the exam papers from the inside pocket of his coat. "What are you going to do with them?" he asked slowly.

Marvin snatched them from him. "Never you mind," he said.

Darren frowned, he couldn't understand why Marvin's attitude towards him had seemed to change. "What about me joining your crew?" he asked.

But none of the crew paid him any mind. They all gathered around Marvin who was flicking through the exam papers feverishly.

"What about me then?" said Darren again, a little more determined.

Darryl Hall looked up from the machine which he had been busy feeding with coins. He walked over to where Darren was standing.

"Look, just because you've got something right for a change doesn't mean you're going to be accepted."

"But I've done what you wanted. What about the party you're having next week? I've got to be there."

Darryl looked at Darren, surprised at his manner. His face tensed and he gritted his teeth. "What's that supposed to mean? Get out of my face," he said, almost spitting out the words. He grabbed Darren by his collar and shoved him onto one of the machines, then turned away to join his friends.

Darren straightened himself up and rubbed his bruised back. He was crestfallen. He now realised that his new-found friends were treating him as they would any other kid in Year 7 or 8. What had he done to deserve such bad treatment? Had they just been using him to get Mr Henry's exam papers?

"Well, remember that you still need me for the last task," he said, turning towards the door.

By this time, the other members of the Smokers' Corner Crew were watching the argument between Darren and Darryl. Daniel Browne, who was Darryl's best friend, started shouting.

"Get outta here! Or do you wanna make something of it?"

Seeing their attitude, Darren thought that it might be in his best interest to leave before the situation got any worse.

"Hey, Cinderella!" Marvin shouted above the noise of the machines. "You'd better get home before you turn into a pumpkin or something."

Darren stepped into the street wondering what he had done to deserve being treated the way he had. He walked towards the bus stop, all the while thinking that perhaps he had made a mistake by mixing with Marvin and the SCC boys.

The next day at school, Tyrone was by himself in the computer room finishing off the design of the magazine. He and Anton and Tenisha had written up most of the articles, but they hadn't yet decided on the name of the magazine.

There was a knock on the door.

"Come in, it's open," said Tyrone, wondering who it could be.

In stepped Remi Oluseyi.

"Oh, hello Remi," said Tyrone. The surprise on his face showed as he stared at the tall, pretty girl standing over him.

Remi's eyes closed into half-slits.

"Don't you 'Hello Remi' me," she said, throwing back her head disdainfully.

Tyrone shuffled uncomfortably in his swivel chair. "Look, if it's about yesterday when we were supposed to meet up at lunch time, I'm really sorry, something came up at the last moment and I couldn't let you know in time. In fact I looked all over for you."

Remi walked slowly towards the windows. "Well, you couldn't have looked very hard is all I can say," she said peering out onto the playground below. "I was standing around for ages."

"Yeah, I can imagine," said Tyrone, trying hard to sound apologetic.

Remi pushed her nose in the air in a superior way. "Well, I won't be asking you to meet me anywhere again."

She walked from the window towards the rows of computers and picked up the copy of the half-finished magazine which Tyrone had been working on.

"Is this what you've been doing?"

Tyrone stood up and walked over to

where Remi was standing.

"Yes, and a lot more," he said.

She threw the papers to one side and swivelled round on her heels. Their noses almost touched as they stood face to face. "Right, I think we had better come straight to the point," she said, looking deep into Tyrone's eyes. "I mean, we can't go on pretending."

Tyrone's heart skipped a beat when he heard this. What did she mean? Surely she didn't mean...?

"I didn't think that you cared," he blurted out, for want of something better to say.

"Of course I care, stupid," she said, looking at him strangely.

Tyrone stared at Remi hard and for the first time realised just how pretty she was. He had previously ignored her because she'd seemed so stush and full of herself. But she seemed somehow different now.

Girls in general didn't seem such a waste of time to Tyrone any longer. He had long forgotten how he used to sum girls up in three sentences: They wear skirts. They cry when they fall over. They can't play football for toffee. Remi's charm was so powerful on him that it was easy for Tyrone to banish such opinions about girls from his mind.

"Do you know that you look really cute?" he said half smiling.

"Yes, I know," she said importantly.

"Would you mind going out with me?" said Tyrone, surprising himself at how easy it came out.

Remi looked at him as if he had gone mad or something. She looked as though she was going to be sick.

"Go out with you?!" she shrieked.

"But, I thought that's what you meant..." stammered Tyrone.

"If you had half a brain cell you'd see that I was talking about Darren," she said, looking at him as if he was a complete fool.

Tyrone was confused. "Oh...yes...of course."

"What I was trying to ask, before you took it upon yourself to dream that I would even remotely consider going out with you," Remi began, regaining her composure, "is, what are we going to do about Darren?"

Tyrone tried to hide his disappointment. For a moment there he had really thought that Remi liked him in the same way she liked his best friend.

"What do you mean?" he asked quietly.

"We've got to get him away from those SCC guys."

Tyrone understood how Remi was feeling. He would have liked to grab Darren by the shirt and shake him so hard that he would remember who his real friends were. He sat down on one of the computer chairs and swivelled around on it.

"Have you tried talking to him?" asked Remi.

"Yes," replied Tyrone, "but I think I've come up with a plan to get him to see sense."

Remi's eyes lit up. Tyrone was rather cute in his own little way. But definitely not 'boyfriend' material. Not for her anyway.

"What did you have in mind?" she asked.

Tyrone stopped swivelling and stood up. He paced about the room with his hands held behind his back like he had seen Mr Robertson do when he was giving one of his lessons. He stroked his chin thoughtfully.

"I'm not fully sure what the plan will be," he said, "but I have a feeling that it will involve the magazine that we're editing."

"Can I help?" Remi asked excitedly, clapping her hands.

"Yes, of course. Tenisha and Anton have to be involved of course," said Tyrone grandly.

"But you just remember," said Remi, wagging her finger at him, "we work on a purely platonic level."

Tyrone scratched his head, his brow was wrinkled as he tried to work out what Remi was on about. "What does 'platonic' mean?"

"I don't know for sure..." said Remi. "I heard it ages ago in a movie and it sounded good at the time. But I think it means we're just friends."

The bell rang to signal the end of break time. Tyrone walked out of the room with Remi. He felt much better after their talk and was confident that, together, they could get Darren back to being the old Darren that they knew and loved.

CHAPTER TEN

The next two days passed without any improvement in Darren's behaviour towards Tyrone and Remi. In fact, Tyrone had tried to telephone him, and Darren's mother, had seemed a little embarrassed when she had to report that Darren had not been home all day. Tyrone had been so concerned about Darren that he asked Remi, Anton and

Tenisha to meet him at the youth centre that evening.

When Tyrone arrived he made straight for the drinks counter and ordered himself a Coke. After paying the lady at the bar he sipped the drink and took a furtive look about. All the regulars were there, and over by the jukebox Patricia was standing, as usual, swinging her hips to the latest song in the charts.

Tyrone nodded in approval when he saw how she was dressed. She looked particularly attractive in her black leggings, white Giorgio top and gold lamé shoes. Her hair was tied into two Pollyanna style pig tails. And although he could not see too clearly from where he was standing, he imagined that she was wearing her hazel-coloured contact lenses.

Tyrone's gaze shifted to the side entrance of the hall. Marvin Johnson and the other members of the SCC were huddled together as usual but he couldn't see whether Darren was with them.

"Tyrone, over here!"

With a start Tyrone turned to see Anton waving to him. Anton was seated by the benches playing dominoes with Tenisha and Remi. Tyrone strolled over to them, drink in hand.

"So, why did you want to meet us here?" asked Tenisha in an excited voice. She had been looking forward to the meeting all day. After all, it wasn't as if anybody ever asked for her company. She removed her spectacles and cleaned them religiously on the sleeve of her black bomber jacket. Her white T-shirt was tucked into luminous pink cycling shorts. She looked totally uncoordinated, with her yellow socks and green-striped trainers. Remi looked more stylish in her black leggings, white ankle socks and white T-shirt. Anton and Tyrone were dressed like most of the other boys in the club: baggy Chipie jeans and denim jackets over American football jackets, and baseball caps pulled low over their eyes.

Tyrone considered what Tenisha was saying. He was not too sure why he had invited them there, but he knew that things had to be sorted quickly or he would lose his best friend. He picked up a basketball from the side of the hall, bounced it a couple of times before he aimed, then threw it towards the net. The ball landed in the middle of the hoop. Tyrone looked pleased with himself. Landing the ball in the centre of the hoop was getting to be child's play.

"I've got a plan," he began, " to use the magazine for a worthwhile purpose."

"What sort of plan?" asked Anton, eyeing Tyrone. He indicated for Tyrone to pass him the ball. Anton bounced the ball and took aim at the backboard. The ball sailed towards the hoop, but, unlike Tyrone's effort, it hit the hoop and landed on Marvin Johnson's head with a thud.

That was the thing with Anton, he sometimes tried too hard to be good at things. But he knew, as did everyone else at Drummond Hill, that he didn't have what it takes to be a Les Ferdinand or a Michael Jordan. He was always one of the last to be picked for any team if, in fact, he was picked at all. There were times when captains would argue that they did not want him on their team, and they would gladly play with one man less than have Anton, 'the liability', in the same side as them. Some kids in Year 7 had even gone so far as to nickname him 'Can't Jump' because he was so hopeless at basketball. And now, it seemed, he had gone too far. The look that Marvin Johnson gave him was not friendly.

"Hey, watch it bwoy! You wanna lose your life?" said Marvin as he threw the ball back with all the strength he could muster. The ball struck Anton squarely on his forehead, jerking his head back with the force. Still reeling, Anton apologised quickly before Marvin had a chance to dream up some more painful punishment. Anton didn't fancy his chances if Marvin decided to start something, and Tyrone, Remi and Tenisha all agreed that Anton did the right thing in apologising, even though Tyrone felt that he overdid the grovelling.

Remi caught the ball before it had the chance to land on their table and upset the game of dominoes. She placed the ball back on the floor.

"What sort of plan do you have in mind?" she asked, hoping that Anton would sit down before he received a thick ear from Marvin Johnson.

"Do you remember that we were looking for a name for the magazine?" Tyrone asked as he searched their faces.

"Yes," Anton replied, guardedly.

"Well, what better name to call it than Focus," said Tyrone with a flourish.

"I agree, that's a wonderful name," Remi said in a superior voice. "But what has that got to do with your plan?"

"I was just coming to that," said Tyrone with rather more drama and suspense in his voice than the situation called for.

"What does 'focus' mean?" asked Anton.

"Looking at something closely," answered Tenisha as she waved her hand dismissively in the air.

"Exactly!" said Tyrone. "That's why we could use the magazine as a way to focus on the Smokers' Corner Crew and others like them."

"Do you mean showing everyone how they bully and tease kids in the lower school?" asked Remi.

"Something like that," Tyrone said grandly. "But you know that we'll have to get the information fast. We only have a couple more weeks to the end of term."

Anton stood, walked round to Tyrone and placed a hand on his shoulder. "Look, I don't want to sound as though I'm chicken," he began. He swallowed hard. "But don't you think that we had better work this out a little more?"

Tyrone looked at Anton blankly. Why was Anton trying to mess up his plan? Everything had been thought out fully. It was simple really: expose the SCC for what they were and they'd stop what they were doing. Then Darren would see them for who they really were: a load of cowardly thugs.

Anton saw Tyrone's confused look. "Imagine what Marvin and his boys would do to us when they find out," he said, nodding to where the gang were.

"So what!" Tyrone blurted. He was fed up

with the attitude that people at the school took. No one ever wanted to get involved in anything against the SCC. Well, he had had enough and he was going to make sure that his best friend was not going to stay in the clutches of the gang any longer.

"I don't know, I just don't know about this," said Anton with reluctance. "I would like to help and all, but if there's any fighting, then I'm outta here."

"I agree with Anton," chirped Tenisha as she anxiously bit her nails.

"Me too," Remi said, standing beside Anton. "But I'm prepared to stand by Tyrone if it means that Darren will finally start to see sense."

"So are we agreed?" Tyrone asked.

There was a moment's silence as the group of friends looked nervously at each other. Then, "Yes," they chorused.

The next day there was a buzz of excitement among everyone in the lower school. Tyrone, Remi, Tenisha and Anton had gone round to all the pupils who they knew had been bullied by Marvin Johnson and his gang. They were surprised to find that there were many more than they'd realised.

Everything seemed to be going well, but they hadn't managed to get anybody to admit, in writing, to being bullied. No one wanted to be known as a squealer. Everyone was too afraid of the consequences. Tyrone was still trying to figure out how to get round this when he met Tenisha outside 8B.

Tenisha had a smile spread across her face. Her eyes bulged, frog-like, from behind her thick-lensed spectacles. She clutched her school bag protectively to her chest.

"It's going really well," she said excitedly.

"I'm not sure," Tyrone said, "I can't get any of them to put their names to anything."

Tenisha scratched her head thoughtfully. Unlike Anton and the rest of the softies at Drummond Hill she didn't get bullied. No one bothered her, they just left her alone on account of all the lies she told. Tenisha could not understand how people got so worked up about a few little exaggerations. For that was how she saw her lies. Little white lies that never hurt anybody.

"We could just write it up using aliases for the people who had been bullied. You know, made-up names — then no one would know who had talked to us."

Tyrone shook his head forcefully even though he was tempted by Tenisha's suggestion. After all, everyone knew that bullying went on, who would care about a few made-up names?

"They'll know who it was," he said eventually.

Tenisha and Tyrone had entered their form room and there was no one about so they went and sat in their seats.

"Anyway, without real names," Tyrone said thoughtfully, "the Smokers' Corner Crew can just deny everything. They would just say that we'd made everything up."

Tenisha placed her head in her arms. She had hoped that everything would be sorted out by now, but it just wasn't going to be that easy.

"So, what shall we do?" she asked with

concern.

"I don't know," sighed Tyrone.

Darren was with Marvin, Roland, Steven and the rest of the SCC outside Mr Patel's sweet shop. This was the moment he had been dreading all term. He suddenly realised that, perhaps, being a member of the SCC was not such a good idea. Marvin and the others were not such nice guys after all, he had discovered. He had been really hurt the other day when they had all laughed at him just because he refused to smoke one of their dope cigarettes. He'd tried to talk his way out of it but someone had grabbed him by the arms and held him while Marvin forced the cigarette into his mouth. He had coughed and spluttered all over the place and become dizzy. They couldn't possibly be good friends, Darren concluded, otherwise they wouldn't have laughed so much when he was being sick all over the pavement afterwards. And as if that hadn't been enough, they'd had a party over the weekend and hadn't even invited him. When he had mentioned it subsequently they had got angry. "You wouldn't have liked it anyway, because there were no rock 'n' roll records," Marvin had said, laughing in his face.

And now they had made him bunk school so he could come and steal with them. Bunking school was bad enough, if his folks got to hear of it, but stealing...! What if he got caught? What if he was arrested and was sent to prison with all those villains? It could even get into the newspapers or, worse, the early evening news; everyone would see his picture. His singing career would be over before it had even begun. The shame of it. He couldn't stand it any longer, he had to get away.

"L...l...look Marvin," he stammered, "I don't think this is a good idea." Darren fought hard to hold back the tears.

Marvin kissed his teeth and gave Darren a hard shove in the back.

"Cho, it's too late to pull out now. You've got to go through with it."

"B...b...but..." Darren stuttered. It had

dawned on him that, assuming the SCC allowed him to join — and he was no longer sure that they would — then he was about to become a fully paid-up member of an exclusive club of criminals. He couldn't help but think about how he had always tried to keep a distance from those kids who stole. 'Teefing' they called it and 'teefing', Darren knew, was wrong. 'Do the right thing', his mother was always telling him, yet he was now moments away from becoming a 'teef'.

"Just think," Roland said, interrupting Darren's train of thought, "after this you'll be down with the in-crowd."

Marvin patted Darren on the back and placed a reassuring arm around his shoulders.

"There's nothing to worry about," he said. "We'll be right behind you."

Darren looked up at him and nodded timidly. "All right, but this is the last thing I'm doing."

"Of course!" shouted the SCC in unison.

With that, Darren was given a shove towards the sweet shop. His knees were knocking and his heart was beating really fast. It sounded like the tom-tom drum of a Native American war party. He suddenly wished that he hadn't dissed Tyrone. Oh, where was his best friend now when he needed him?

As he stepped into the newsagents the bell rang. Darren's heart thumped harder.

There were two shoppers already inside, one of whom was being served by Mr Patel. The Asian shopkeeper looked up as Darren walked in. The stare that he gave him made Darren's heart skip a beat. Mr Patel seemed to know why he had come into the shop. It was as if there was a huge sign across his forehead saying, 'TEEF'. Darren made to the section where the chocolates were, his hands trembling. It felt as though there were eyes peering at him from every corner of the shop.

It's now or never, Darren thought to himself. He counted eight bars of chocolate into his trouser pockets, four in each one, and headed swiftly towards the door. He'd done it. He breathed a heavy sigh of relief as he stepped out of the door.

It was then that he felt the heavy hand on his shoulder. He spun around to see the scowling face of Mr Patel.

"Oh no!" Darren cried. "I'm really done for now."

Terror shone in Darren's eyes and all he could think of was gaining his freedom and liberty. In his panic he managed to shake himself free of the shopkeeper's grasp, and made a dash for the street. It was only then that he saw, to his amazement, Marvin, Roland and the others making off down the High Street as fast as their legs would carry them. Darren made off after them with Mr Patel in hot pursuit.

Hey stop!" cried the shopkeeper. "I know who you are!"

Darren had reached the curb when he saw Sabre, the terrier, come bounding towards him. Darren turned to dodge past him but was too late to avoid tripping over the pavement. He fell, banging his head, and remained on the ground with Sabre gripping the bottom of his trouser leg between his teeth and snarling at him. Every dog has its day, and today was Sabre's day.

CHAPTER ELEVEN

"So, what's happening?" Tyrone asked as he tried to wake his friend by tickling the end of his feet.

Darren turned to face him, all drowsy still.

"Unhh?!" he said, wiping the sleep from his eyes. His face lit up when he recognised his smiling friend.

For the past two days since he'd been at

home with his head cut open and his ribs bruised, Darren had been worrying about Tyrone. He had gone over in his mind all that had happened since the beginning of term, particularly the way he had treated Tyrone over recent weeks. He was ashamed about how he had dissed his best friend in favour of Marvin and the rest, especially since it was Tyrone who had rescued him from the pavement outside Mr Patel's shop.

Darren hated himself for not listening to Tyrone's advice about smoking cigarettes, and he had thought long and hard about why he had started bunking school. As he lay with his head swathed in bandages and his front tooth missing - so that when he smiled he looked like Goofy - the arcade and the SCC did not have their previous allure.

Tyrone smiled reassuringly at his friend. "Does your head hurt?" he asked simply.

"Not much," Darren replied. "Though you'd better not make me laugh because it kills my ribs." Darren picked up one of the comics that Tyrone had brought with him. "Not that I've been laughing much recently," he added.

They were silent for a moment.

"I was thinking..." Darren said suddenly.

"What?" asked Tyrone, popping a grape into his mouth.

"I was thinking that I must seem like such a fool."

Tyrone stopped eating. He spat out the grape pips into the palm of his hand and threw them into the wastepaper basket under the bed.

"What?"

"I should have known better," Darren continued. "I should never have hung about with Marvin and his boys."

By the look on Darren's face Tyrone could see that he had learnt a very painful lesson. It wouldn't have been fair to gloat over his friend's misfortunes. As far as Tyrone was concerned, nothing Darren had said or done would change things between them. He was happy to live and let live.

"It's all right."

"No Ty, I was such a fool. I've been so dumb."

"Do you know that you can use your experience in a positive way?" Tyrone said, walking around the bed importantly as he talked.

"What are you on about?"

"Remember the magazine?"

"Yeah."

"Well, why don't you write something about what it's like lying at home in bed, getting grapes and watching daytime TV when you should be at school."

"You mean like no homework and all that?"

"That's right."

"Would you really like me to?" Darren said in a low voice. He badly needed to do something for Tyrone, to pay him back for standing by him.

"Of course I would," said Tyrone. "After all we're best friends."

Best friends.

Throughout his nightmare period with the SCC, Darren had forgotten what 'best friends' really meant. He had gone around with an air of big-headedness not paying any

165

attention to his real friend, all the while thinking that standing by the bike sheds would make him a better person. How could he have been so stupid?

"Thanks, you're the best mate anyone could wish for," he said, turning to face Tyrone.

"I don't know how I'm ever going to pay you back for getting me away from Mr Patel's."

Darren recalled the moment, two days before, when Tyrone had come to his rescue only just in time. There he had been, lying helpless on the ground, trapped between a snarling Sabre and a furious Mr Patel, when Tyrone suddenly appeared. He had been out of breath from running, but still managed to aim a sharp kick at Sabre. The dog had been so shocked that he disappeared into a neighbouring garden, howling as he went.

The next thing Darren knew, Tyrone was picking him up off the floor. "You owe me £1.60 for the chocolate bars," he had said angrily, as they had hobbled down the road together.

"I've got them in my pocket," Darren remembered saying. "Why didn't you just give them back?"

"Because I thought the money was a more honest thing to do. Anyway, I needed to convince him that you'd been bullied into taking the chocolate and that your real friends always paid their way."

"Did he believe you?"

Tyrone shot Darren a withering look a look that had haunted Darren ever since.

"And now," Tyrone had continued, "we're going back to your place and I'm going to save your neck again by telling your mum that you fell over in the school playground. The teachers never really watch, so they'll probably believe it. Then you'll just have to pray that no one except Anton saw you bunking off with the SCC."

Darren looked now at Tyrone, as he sat on the edge of the bed. "Is that how you knew where I'd gone?" he asked.

"What?" said Tyrone, who couldn't read Darren's mind.

"When Anton saw me leaving school the

other day? Is that how you knew I was going to be in trouble?"

Tyrone shrugged his shoulders. "I guessed," he said.

"But how did you know that I was at Mr Patel's?" asked Darren, who had only just thought of this.

"I got out of school quick enough to follow you," Tyrone replied. "Though you and your homies were making so much noise I could probably have heard you from halfway across town."

"Oh," Darren mumbled. Then he suddenly realised what Tyrone had said. "You got out of school." He was shocked. "You bunked off." He was horrified. Tyrone would never have dreamed of doing that if it hadn't have been for Darren's stupid behaviour. "How did you get out of class?" he asked, his eyes wide.

"I told Miss Bird I needed to go to the toilet," Tyrone answered. "Just like someone else did in geography a couple of weeks ago."

"Oh, yes," Darren remembered. "They

said I had to," he added, sheepishly.

"It was you who let off the fire extinguishers, wasn't it?" Tyrone tried to sound serious, but his mouth twitched into a smile.

"Yes," said Darren, grinning.

"I knew it was you," Tyrone giggled. "Mr Fredricks looks better with a purple face, doesn't he?" and they both fell about laughing, with Darren shouting, "Stop!" or "Oh no!" every five seconds, as he held his aching ribs.

At last they were both able to calm down and Darren offered his fist to Tyrone. They touched.

"Thanks, man," Darren said, quietly.

"No trouble." Tyrone smiled. "It's just good to have you back."

At school the following day, Tyrone was walking on air. He had finally got his best friend back and Darren had promised to help with the magazine. He walked along the corridor after lunch, towards the boys' toilets. He was feeling elated, but his face fell when he saw Marvin Johnson blocking his way as he made to walk up the stairs. Tyrone moved to one side, trying to avoid contact with the older boy. He didn't want to give Marvin the excuse to pick a fight with him.

"Where do you think you're going?" asked Marvin brusquely.

"Upstairs."

"I know that, stupid," Marvin said, shoving Tyrone in the chest. "I hear that you're writing a magazine?"

"What of it?" answered Tyrone, pushing his way past.

Putting the thumb and index finger of his right hand in his mouth, Marvin blew a shrill whistle. As if from nowhere, Steven, Roland and the other members of the SCC stepped from behind the lockers at the top of the stairs. Tyrone stopped dead in his tracks and tensed his muscles, ready to defend himself.

Marvin Johnson grabbed Tyrone by the collar and pushed him to the wall, causing his head to bang against it.

"We don't want to see any silly gossip in it. Do we?" he spat menacingly.

Tyrone didn't answer. He stared defiantly at his aggressor.

"Do we?" Marvin repeated, slamming Tyrone against the wall again.

Tyrone nodded. He'd heard what the SCC did to people who didn't heed their threats.

When he was sure that Tyrone had got the message Marvin let go of him, but not without a swift kick to the backside to make sure that Tyrone didn't forget. Then he nodded to his associates and they headed out of the hall into the playground.

Tyrone, smarting, pulled himself together, rubbing his bottom. He made his way up the remaining stairs crying, not from the kick he'd received, but out of frustration that he had let the SCC walk all over him. He went to the boys' toilet where he washed away his tears. Straightening his tie, he removed any evidence that he'd had an altercation.

However, it wasn't as easy to hide the look of misery in his eyes which remained with him for the rest of the day.

After school, Remi came running up to Tyrone. Tenisha and Anton were close behind.

"Are you okay?" Remi asked, in a concerned tone.

"Of course. Why shouldn't I be?"

"Look, we know what happened," said Tenisha.

"Robert Collins saw it all and told us," Anton added.

"Don't worry, they won't get away with it," Remi said forcefully. She had finally decided that the time was right to get tough with the SCC. They'd had no right bashing Tyrone like they did. He hadn't done anything to them. They had no right to bash anyone in. What's more, they had conspired to get Darren in trouble too. She knew that she would have to act fast if her plan was going to work.

"It's time we wrote about them in the magazine," Remi continued. "And we don't need any of the other kids to tell about them. We've suffered enough from them ourselves, and I'm not afraid to say it."

"And I'm not afraid to put my name to it," said Tyrone, and the two of them slapped a high five.

CHAPTER TWELVE

Darren was back at school the following week — although he hobbled about a bit. The first issue of Focus had already come out when he returned to school and everyone was pleased that there was now a magazine which dealt with issues concerning them. A lot of interest was shown in the article on bullying. Tyrone had written a colourful account of what went on in the school. He talked about how the barriers between teachers and pupils needed to be broken down before kids could feel safe about reporting bullying. Then he had named the members of the SCC and written in detail about what they had been doing. He described how they 'taxed' the lower school for using the bike sheds and how they lured younger kids into stealing for them. And then Tyrone signed his name at the bottom of the piece. It was an act of true courage.

Following the publication of that first issue of the magazine, Mr Fredricks had called a special assembly. Marvin Johnson was there and hissed at Tyrone when he walked past, "I'm going to get you."

Tyrone ignored him. It had been so funny when Mr Fredricks called the Smokers' Corner Crew one by one onto the platform and pulled their ears in front of everybody. The teachers had known that there was bullying, but had never had the evidence to pin on Marvin and his cronies. Since seeing Tyrone's article they'd been taking more notice of the Smokers' Corner Crew. Mr Fredricks himself had even caught them harassing one of the Year 7 pupils.

After the assembly the whole school came out into the playground expecting a fight. Word had spread like wild-fire that Tyrone was going to get his face mashed up. And when Tyrone eventually emerged from the assembly hall, a large circle formed around him. He could clearly see Marvin, Roland, Steven and the other members of the SCC standing in a line, staring at him menacingly. Tyrone glanced at each of them in turn. From the looks on their faces, they weren't messing about. He felt afraid.

Marvin took a couple of steps towards him. The ear pulling in front of the whole school was a humiliation he could not forgive. Someone was going to pay for it. Now those silly little lower school children were threatening to stop paying tax for parking their bikes by the sheds. All because of that stupid magazine.

"You're finished yout'!" Marvin said glaring.

Tyrone couldn't answer. He was paralysed with fear and knew he didn't stand a chance in a fight with the SCC. Marvin took another step forward and grabbed Tyrone by the shoulder.

"Hold it!"

Marvin spun around. Standing in front of him was a defiant Remi Oluseyi. She'd rounded up the whole lower school when she had heard that the SCC were going to punish Tyrone for the article and had coaxed and pleaded with pupils to support him in his efforts to banish the bullies from Drummond Hill. After all, it was for their good that Tyrone had risked a beating from the SCC by exposing them in the magazine. It wasn't fair to let him get whupped without helping him.

"Oh, he's brought the petticoat brigade!" Marvin laughed when he saw Remi. He took a long drag from his rolled up cigarette and blew it menacingly towards the angry girl.

Remi screwed up her face as the odour wafted towards her, then she placed two fingers in her mouth and let out a shrill whistle.

From behind the bike sheds came Robert Collins, the Year 7 kid who was always being bullied by the SCC.

"What's this then?" Steven said laughing, "Weaklings United?" He went and stood next to Marvin. He was going to back his crew member up if necessary. Who did these dumb kids think they were? The SCC were the toughest and strongest gang in the school.

And Marvin was confident too. With his crew around him he knew he could handle anything and anybody.

Remi placed her fingers in her mouth a second time and blew. Jason Frickley, a boy in her year, stepped out from the middle of the crowd. Marvin and the SCC had bullied him so much that he'd started to believe all the things that they'd said about him.

"Cho!" said Roland kissing his teeth. "I'm going to mash all your faces. I'm going to rearrange them for you!" He didn't like the way things seemed to be turning, but there were eight of them against three little boys and a girl. He'd show them who was boss and they'd each get a taste of his speciality kung fu kick, that was for sure.

Tyrone, like all the boys at school, knew about Roland's speciality kick and the fact that he regarded flushing his victim's heads down the toilets afterwards as some kind of a joke.

Remi stepped forward and stood beside Tyrone. He looked at her and they exchanged a smile. She let out two further loud whistles. Anton and Darren stepped out from behind Jason.

"Are you going to apologise?" Anton asked, wagging a finger at Marvin and his boys. He remembered that day at the youth centre when Marvin had burst the bubble in his trainers. It had been one of the worst days in his life. Yet the SCC had rolled around with laughter at his discomfort. Only Tyrone had come to his aid at the time and he owed it to his friend to stand by him now.

Darren hobbled over towards Marvin and the rest of the SCC.

"Yes, apologise, scum," he said, pointing angrily at Marvin.

"You pathetic little creep, James. Did you really think we would make you a member of the SCC? We were just using you. Now kiss the world goodbye," Marvin spat, clenching and unclenching his fists as he walked towards Anton.

Remi whistled a final time and the main doors opened. Out into the playground streamed over sixty children in Year 7 and 8, who had all been bullied at some time or other by the SCC.

Marvin and his gang looked at each other nervously.

"People like you should be ashamed of yourselves," said Tyrone, when he saw the crowd gathering behind him. "And do you know what has really started to get up my nose?" he said, wagging a menacing finger at the SCC.

None of the gang answered. But they shifted their feet nervously.

"You and all your crew," Tyrone continued, "hanging around and thinking you're something."

"Yeah," said Darren, who was still dangerously close to the SCC. "You think you're so clever smoking cigarettes and weed and stuff," he continued defiantly.

Marvin and his friends exchanged embarrassed looks and glanced around shiftily.

"You think it's cool to hang around the arcade with red eyes, saying 'you know what I mean', when in reality you don't even know what time it is, let alone what you mean?" Darren went on, warming to his theme.

"That's right," interrupted Remi. "You might think you're cool, but to everyone else you just look mash up."

It was true. Remi had given it a great deal of thought and remembered how Darren had been when he started hanging around the SCC. It had made her so angry. She remembered how her older brother and some of his friends had started to mess with dope a couple of years before, and next thing they knew their grades had started to drop and they lost interest in school. It had got so bad that her brother even stopped going to school altogether. All he was interested in was where his next spliff was coming from.

"Outlaws like us have been around for years and will never go away," said Marvin courageously, urging his crew on. He stepped forward and grabbed Darren by the collar.

The first punch hit Marvin full in the face. Tyrone looked around to see who had thrown it. Standing to his side with his sleeves rolled up, was Tony Mensah, the big brother in Year 12.

"Argh!" cried Marvin as he was sent reeling, his face stinging with pain.

"And that's just for starters," said Tony, slipping his school blazer back on. "You touch any of these kids again and you'll get more trouble than you'll ever be able to handle...and that goes for the rest of you fools," he added, with a dismissive wave of his hand at the SCC. "Now get out of my sight before I get really mad."

Marvin started crying. Tony's punch reminded Tyrone of when he had seen Frank Bruno get beaten in the boxing ring by Mike Tyson. It didn't matter how 'bad' you considered yourself, there was always someone 'badder' than you. Marvin looked around him to see his friends running out of the school gates. He was alone.

"I'll get you for this," Marvin told Tyrone tearfully, but everyone knew he was only making up noise.

"No, you will not," said Mr Singh as he came into the playground. "Here's a letter that I'm sending to your parents telling them that you have been suspended from Drummond Hill."

There was a loud cheer from all around as Marvin was led out of the school by his shirt collar.

Tyrone turned to Remi, who was standing next to him, and said, "I don't know how you did it, but thanks."

"No, we owe you one, Tyrone. If you didn't come up with the idea of exposing the bullying in the magazine we would still all be at the mercy of the SCC," said Remi. "I guess sometimes you have to fight for what's right and damn the consequences." Then she added light-heartedly. "But we could have

182

bashed them in without Tony Mensah."

"That's right," said Tenisha, appearing as if from nowhere. "I was just getting ready to smash Marvin in the face," she lied.

"Yeah, right," said Remi, winking at Tyrone and Darren once more.

TYRONE'S GUIDE FOR PUPILS OF OTHER SCHOOLS

JUST FOLLOW THIS SIMPLE GLOSSARY, AND THE WORLD OF THE DRUMMOND HILL CREW WILL OPEN BEFORE YOU.

---

bad bwoy A boy who acts tough and macho.
bigga Any big person.
bigging up his chest Being boastful.
blouse an' skirt An exclamation.
bro Term of endearment used to a close male friend.
buck up Get together or meet up.
butters Ugly, unsightly.
cho An expression of nonchalance.
crew Group of people or a gang.
criss Looking good/nice/sharp.
cuff A blow with a fist or hand.
dem Caribbean patois word meaning 'They'.
dissin'/to diss Ignoring or embarrassing somebody.
easy nuh Careful/take it easy.
got a handle To like someone a lot, to fancy them, to have the 'hots' for them.
gunga peas Caribbean dish consisting of beans.
homie/homegirl/homeboy Term used to denote a close friend.

Jackson Five Famous 70s family group - Michael Jackson was once with the group.

Jeez An exclamation.

Jodeci A popular soul group.

laters Goodbye/Catch you later.

licks A beating or a slap.

making up noise Shouting or boasting.

mash up Rough. Messy. Unsuitable.

'nuff dollars Loads of money.

nutmegged Football expression meaning, to kick the ball through the opponent's legs.

respect 1 Hello or Goodbye. Greeting used amongst close friends. 2. To give someone genuine praise.

ride Bothering somebody.

seen 1.Understanding a message. 2. Agreeing with someone-. 3. Yes.

slam dunk Basketball term meaning, to hit the ball violently through the basket.

skank to pull a fast one.

sneakers American term for Trainers.

spars Close friends.

stush Stuck-up/Snobbish.

sweet 1. Happy. 2. Nice. 3. Fine.

teef/teefing A thief /The act of stealing.

yout Youngster.

The X Press invites you to join the

DRUMMOND HILL CREW

Book Club

Write to us about the books you enjoyed and tell us about your favourite characters.

Keep updated with the news from Drummond Hill by sending your name and address to:

The Drummond Hill Crew Book Club
The X Press
6 Hoxton Square
London N1 6NU
Tel: 0171 729 1199

LIVIN' LARGE

New boy Junior Brown arrives at Drummond Hill School dressed in the latest designer clothes and with enough money to buy all the friends he'll ever need. Junior quickly becomes the most popular boy in his year, but makes an enemy of Darren James when Remi, Darren's girl, takes an interest in the new boy. What's more, Junior has replaced him in the school basketball team. To Darren, Junior is acting too big for his boots and is a show-off, so he decides to investigate. If he can find out where the new boy is getting all his money from, he'll be able to expose him as bogus and get back his popularity, his place in the basketball team and his girl. But Junior isn't what he seems and Darren ends up discovering more than he bargained for.

ISBN 1-874509-34-4

The **DRUMMOND HILL CREW** Series

AGE AIN'T NOTHING BUT A NUMBER

When some of the pupils from Drummond Hill go on a school trip to the mysterious Headstone Manor, they find themselves right in the middle of an adventure! Are the strange noises in the night really made by a ghost?

ISBN 1-874509-33-6